What others have said about Rites of Passage for Teens:

"This volume is a beautifully elegant tribute to both the historical veracity and practical effectiveness of the well known but little understood Bar and Bat mitzvah rituals. Weaving together spiritual significance and deep insight into the nature of young men and women and the challenges they face, this book could enrich your family life for generations." -- **Rabbi Daniel Lapin, President,** *American Alliance of Jews and Christians*

"As the student minister for Hunter's two oldest daughters I am so excited that he is sharing his passion for passing on his faith to his family through symbols, traditions, and ceremonies that make it impossible for his children to miss the blessings God has for them. Both of these girls are amazing young women. They walk through life with the confidence of the blessing of their earthly father and the security of knowing their identity given to them by their Heavenly Father. If you put into practice what you read in this book you will go a long way toward seeing the same happen in your teenager." -- **Jeremy Lee, Student Minister, New Vision Baptist Church, Murfreesboro, TN**

"In a world falling apart, it becomes all the more important to be rooted and grounded in the love of God and in a healthy family environment. Hunter has done us a great service by bringing Jewish traditions into the Christian camp. I have used these practices he shares in this wonderful book in my own family and have seen fruit that remains. Blessings to you as you read this strategic book and implement what Hunter offers into the life of your family." -- **James W. Goll, Encounters Network, Prayer Storm, Compassion Acts; Author of The Seer, The Lost Art of Intercession; widower, father of four**

"We all struggle in trying to figure out the best ways to raise our children in the fear of God so that they know His love, feel His mercy, and live in His presence. *Rites of Passage for Teens* is a very timely book filled with tried and true wisdom written by a man who has lived it. I have watched Hunter live out his faith in very practical ways over the years and know him to be faithful, loving, and sincere. This book will certainly change the way I approach my own children's passage into adulthood. It holds an excellent yet simple solution for a very vexing problem. My recommendation? Read it." -- **Omar L. Hamada, MD, Medical Director for Pregnancy Support Center, Murfreesboro, TN, faithfully married fifteen years, father of four children**

"As a youth pastor, with Hunter McFarlin's leadership, we implemented a series of church-wide blessing ceremonies during our tenure. In every single case, the event was an astounding success. Every young adult vividly remembers their special night (even those held six years ago). By the end of every one of the ceremonies, the parents were blessed, the honored young men and women were blessed, and the siblings were blessed. Each person came away proud of the evening and looking forward to the next ceremony for a sibling or friend. For many families, this event released tongues of blessing spoken by the parents over their children. And watching other parents love on their children inspired me to love my children more demonstrably. The prophecies, prayers, and blessings spoken brought laughter, smiles and many tears. The events were truly sweet times, and the impact the events had cannot be measured. Nearly all of those families who started the tradition have continued to include all of their other children. I hold this as proof of the power the ceremony released for the participants." -- **David Ives, father of six, faithfully married twenty-two years**

"Having identical twin boys is more than a double blessing for us. Even though they look the same, we knew early on that each one was uniquely fashioned by God. We always treated them as individuals, and when it came time for their 'rite of passage' our desire was for them to be publicly affirmed as men and not just as 'the twins.' This ceremony was a great moment in their lives. We continue to celebrate them and are so proud of them, now both honor students in their respective universities. Thank you, Hunter, for leading us in this important aspect of their lives." -- **Bud Zegel, father of five children, faithfully married twenty-nine years**

"We live in a time and culture where elders imitate youth rather than guide them; where sageing has been replaced with mere aging. What we need is a new respect for the wisdom gleaned from a life long lived, and rites of passage for our youth that ground them in that wisdom. Hunter McFarlin has done us a great service with his new book offering guidance to moms and dads in how to honor their teens with rituals that will help them see the the promise of growing up as righteous and compassionate citizens of the world." -- **Rabbi Rami Shapiro, author of** *Recovery, the Sacred Art: The Twelve Steps as Spiritual Practice*

"I'm not a reader, and I have no children. But I began reading *Rites of Passage for Teens* and was pulled in and could not stop until I had read every word on every page. I loved everything about the book, and I was emotionally affected by various parts -- why? Because I realized that I missed this process in my childhood and afterwards. I feel the loss." -- **Dan Davis, retired accountant, faithfully married forty-six years**

"Hunter has put together an approach for recognizing and supporting a transition to adulthood that is meaningful and biblical. It was a watershed in the lives of our children, and I highly recommend both Hunter and this approach to you." -- **Andy Reese, Author of Freedom Tools, father of four, faithfully married 27 years**

"In a culture that is usually split by differences, Hunter has done the impossible: he's written a guide that parents and children alike can encounter together; that both laymen and professionals can embrace enthusiastically. He combines the practical and the substantial, which have been developed by his living them out. Writing with a parent's heart, Hunter has a directness in his style that is extremely engaging and makes this a most valuable resource for anyone who is a parent or a son/daughter, or anyone who works with them. We recommend this book most enthusiastically." -- **Dr. William and Jean Penrod, retired, Department of Psychology, Middle Tennessee State University**

My wife and I, with our six incredible children, attended the same church as the McFarlins when Hunter first proposed the idea for a "Bar Baraka" dinner and celebration. I had no idea what that was, but we decided to participate with our oldest child, who was thirteen at the time. I never knew what an impact that would have on him and on us as a family. I can say now, after having the first four of our six children blessed in a public way through a rite of passage blessing ceremony, and also openly observing other important times in their lives, that what Hunter advocates in this book is life changing for them and for our family as a whole. These events in your family life will prove irreplaceable. Don't miss them. In this day and age of families fracturing and children in trouble, Hunter offers a life-giving message. -- **Tod Bell, CEO, Our Mission Network International**

"As a Jew and as a parent of two teenagers, I am interested in *Rites of Passage for Teens* for several reasons. Foremost, it seeks to spread Jewish wisdom surrounding a precious Jewish ritual, the Bar and Bat mitzvah. I honor Hunter's goal to spread the wisdom of blessing the passage from childhood to adulthood. When we take time for this blessing, I believe it honors a Jewish mission to be a 'light unto the nations,' and creates stronger families with healthier communities. May this work honor the integrity of Judaism and spread this wisdom into Christian communities in a way that does not seek to replace Jewish ritual, but rather creates a unique Christian ritual." -- **Martin Sir, Esq., Secretary of Temple O'habai Shalom, Nashville, TN**

Rites of Passage for Teens

A parent's guide to navigating

every child's transition

into adulthood

Rites of Passage for Teens

A parent's guide to navigating

every child's transition

into adulthood

Hunter McFarlin

ISBN # 978-0-9829263-0-7

MALACHI 4 PUBLISHING, LLC

www.huntermcfarlin.com

I dedicate this book to Jeremy Lee, creator of *www.ritesofpassageproject.com* for families at New Vision Baptist Church, Murfreesboro, Tennessee.

May the Lord use this resource to help families, churches, schools, cities, and nations to embrace rites of passage ceremonies for blessing teenagers into adulthood for the Glory of God.

Special thanks to Hal Sandifer, Steve Bates, Steve Goostree, Dr. Richard A. Ross, Steve Geyer, and New Vision Baptist Church for making Jeremy's dream come true! Jabez prayer for all of you, in Jesus' name. Amen.

www.ritesofpassageproject.com

Listen, my child:

> God the Father will always be present for you,
>   mighty to save.
> He gladly finds his joy in you!
>   With his love, he calms all your fears.
> Your Father God dances over you, singing joyful songs!

- Zephaniah 3:17 (paraphrased)

Contents

Acknowledgements

When I was 18, I left home as a superficial, insecure, impulsive, argumentative and ungrateful college freshman (just ask my parents!). Yet, I was devout in my hunger to know God, learn His ways and walk in them. It was Professor Bill Penrod, a former Baptist pastor, and his wife, Jean, who were both truly pastoring college students as psychology professors at Middle Tennessee State University, who first introduced me to the value of rites of passage. Dr. Penrod, or Bill, as he prefers to be called, had such an impact on me that I enrolled in every class he offered. He taught a lot about parenting in his "Personality and Adjustment" class. We studied rites of passage in cultures around the world in "Adolescent Psychology." I was intrigued by the eleven common parenting methods shared by homes that produced "highly intelligent or creative people," which we studied in his class, "Creativity and Intelligence." His classes and assignments gave me invaluable insights into myself and into parenting. Almost daily, I think of something I learned from Bill and Jean. Eternal thanks to both of you.

Linette and I were members of a new church in Franklin, Tennessee, Abounding Grace Church, almost from its inception in 1992 until we moved away in 2003. Some of the leaders were David and Peggy Fitzpatrick, Bill and Carolan Lee (deceased), Andy and Susan Reese, Brian and Sue Smallwood, Buddy and Eileen Zegel, David and Tina DeLoach, Mark and Bev Elliott, and many other faithful people who had a profound influence on our marriage, our parenting, and our walk with God. These leaders and our friends at Abounding Grace walked us out of childishness into maturity. The congregation embraced us and our desire to see our children grow up in a culture of coming of age, rites of passage ceremonies. Most of what we have experienced first hand with rites of passage was with Abounding Grace Church families. Thank you Abounding Grace!

Karen Dean, a pastor of Belmont Church in the early 1990's, was an influential teacher of the Scriptures in our lives during the time of our first pregnancy and Heather Grace's birth. She taught us to love the Hebrew Scriptures (Old Testament) and understand them as God's story for raising His own "teenager," Israel. Thank you, Karen. Heather has become a wise and beautiful young adult now, with two younger sisters and a younger brother nipping at her heels. We are some of the living epistles you have written this side of the final rite of passage! Thank you.

Marty and Jenny Goetz and Anthony and Mary Keith Skinner were significant contributors to our own blessing ceremonies for Heather (the Goetz's) and Mary Anna (the Skinner's). Thank you, Marty and Jenny, for your example of celebrating the Jewishness of Jesus and Christianity. Your music remains a significant influence in our home and inspired Heather to request "a Marty Goetz concert" for her blessing ceremony. Your contributions significantly aided me in putting aside my "first-timer-trepidations" in blessing Heather and validated my desires to be a little more like my "natural born" Jewish brethren. I hope I can live in and enjoy the goodness of God as passionately as you two.

Anthony Skinner - my friend who sticks closer than a brother, thank you for over 20 years of "healing for damaged emotions" and for helping Heather take her first steps. Thank you for raising Mary Anna's blessing ceremony to a poignant level of unforgettable validation for her and us. Thank you for clinging to the path of life with Mary Keith and raising wise and beautiful children – wonderful friends to Elisha and Esther. You and Mary Keith are "shining example" parents and very dear friends. Because you are here, I hope the Lord tarries and we live to our 100's.

Jeremy Lee, Student Minister, facilitates an amazing culture of worship, adventure, and community for young adults at New Vision Baptist Church, Murfreesboro, Tennessee. Thank you, Jeremy, for inviting me to be a contributor to New Vision's rites of passage website (*www.ritesofpassageproject.com*) and for launching the writing of this book! Thank you also for leading a rich and supportive faith community for my teenage daughters. You and Beth sow faithfulness in the lives of hundreds of budding young adults and families. Your singular focus inspires me. May the Lord continue to enrich your harvest.

Frank Shepard Midgley, III -- your friendship and your family's move to Murfreesboro significantly contributed to the validation within me that led to this book. We are all on a journey with more questions than answers. The extent of love and respect between us, in the midst of credible disagreements, is uplifting and rare. I feel your love. Thank you.

Dr. Richard A. Ross (*www.richardaross.com*), author of *True Love Waits*, inspired me to believe that I have a valid place among the voices of encouragement to parents. Your book, *30 Days*, has been a valuable guide for me in having authentic dialogue with my own teenagers. While we were together, it was both what you said and didn't say that provided me with clarification in my role as a father and as a son.

From 1997 to 1999 I repeatedly attended Craig Hill *Ancient Paths* seminars and read his books. More than any author, Craig Hill molded my understanding and targeted my passion for rites of passage ceremonies. Chapter three of this book is my recollection of Craig Hill material. I highly recommend his *Ancient Paths* seminars and his books *Bar Barakah, Ancient Paths,* and *Wealth, Riches and Money* (*www.familyfoundations.com*).

Authors such as, Bill Ligon (*Imparting the Blessing, www.thefathersblessing.com*), Gordon Dalbey (*Healing the Masculine Soul, www.abbafather.com*), John Sheasby (*Son!, www.liberatedliving.com*), John Eldredge (*Wild At Heart, www.ransomedheart.com*), Neil Anderson (*Bondage Breaker, Victory over Darkness, www.ficm.org*), Rabbi Daniel Lapin (*Thou Shall Prosper, www.rabbidaniellapin.com*), Kris Vallotton (*The Father's Blessing, www.kvministries.com*), David Seamands (*Healing for Damaged Emotions*), have all had profound influence in my life.

When I was six years old, I asked my father "Dad, how did you find Mom?" Early in life, I longed for an excellent woman. Linette Bitzer is God's gift to me. Thank you Tommye and Georgiana for raising a lovely and remarkable woman. Thank you Linette for finding me. Thank you for loving me. You are my true partner, companion, friend, and lover. You believe in me more than I believe in myself. You confront me more than I confront myself. You are the evidence that I am richly favored by God.

Thank you. "Like berries on the vine…"

Heather, Mary Anna, Elisha, and Esther -- wow, what a crew! Am I really your dad? You guys are amazing. Thank you for forgiving me when I am mean. Thank you for celebrating with me when I win. Thank you for trusting me. Thank you for praying for me and pulling for me. You honor me. Heather delivers. Mary Anna creates. Elisha comforts. Esther delights. You are my favorite people to be with.

Freddy Richardson, my editor. Thank you for helping my concepts become a book! Congratulations on your rich marriage and your children's successes! You raise me up.

Mom and Dad, Larry and Maryedith McFarlin -- it's all your fault ☺! Much of who I am today is the result of your life. I hope I make you proud. Thank you for all you have given and continue to give.

Introduction

What does a teenager need in order to prosper? What can a parent do to help teenagers choose wisely?

As of the writing of this book (Summer 2010), my wife, Linette, and I have been married for twenty-one years. We have four children. Heather is eighteen. Mary Anna is fourteen. Elisha Luke is nine. Esther is five. All are delightful people. They are happy and confident. The teenage years in our home have been mostly a wonderful experience -- even with a strong-willed eighteen year old! Our children show respect to adults and to one another. They are diligent. Our kindergartener, third grader, and eighth grader are students in advanced magnet schools. Our oldest daughter graduated as president of her student body in a public high school with 2,600 students. She has been awarded academic scholarships from prestigious universities.

They are loving and helpful people. They are influential among their peers. They respect each other, even in the midst of conflict. Our teenage daughters actively choose their own involvement in worship and church attendance, as well as private Bible reading and prayer. They walk in their own personal faith in God, following in the footsteps of their parents. Linette and I help them, but they make wise choices of their own volition.

While my family and I are Christians, we value many Jewish traditions. We have celebrated Jewish holidays and traditions since Heather was three years old. As followers of Jesus, our family values the godliness and wisdom found in Jewish culture. Periodically over the last fifteen years, Linette and I have received sincere inquiries from teachers, coaches, ballet instructors, and others, such as "What do you do?," and "How do you do it?," regarding the parenting of our remarkable children. We believe that our incorporation of rites of passage and blessing ceremonies in our family is one of the primary answers to these questions.

In sharing the pre-press copy of this book with a number of Christian and Jewish leaders, I have had sincere dialogue with folks from both religions who have voiced a few legitimate concerns regarding this book. It has been a wonderful learning process for me. In fact, in some ways, this book will remain a work in progress. Though you have here a finished book, a new edition may soon replace this one with significant updates, which I welcome! I have endeavored to write a book about parenting which can be endorsed by the rabbi and the pastor, by Jews and Christians alike, and which can be used effectively by parents of teenagers within any religious tradition.

This book is not intended to spread religious beliefs or to merge Judaism and Christianity. My goal is to encourage wise parenting and to offer specific ways in which to do it. I believe ALL parents of teenagers, whether Jewish or Christian or any other faith background, can benefit from developing their own family traditions of rites of passage and from reading this book.

Perhaps this book will awaken Christian families to the benefits of the Jewish traditions of Bar and Bat mitzvah. Perhaps this book will awaken some Jewish families to the richness of their own ancient ritual with a renewed vigor for their traditions. While a Bar or Bat mitzvah cannot be performed without a rabbi, any family can glean the wisdom and value of this Jewish tradition and incorporate their own coming of age, rite of passage ceremony and celebration.

"Jews have prospered in every country and in every century," Rabbi Daniel Lapin said in his influential book, *Thou Shall Prosper*.[1] One of the reasons for this prosperity is the Bar/Bat mitzvah – a coming of age rite of passage ceremony.

By the word *prosperity* I mean wholeness and competence. Personal wholeness includes being integrated (as opposed to being scattered or fractured), being grounded, internally structured, rooted -- possessing clarity of one's identity. Personal competence includes being trustworthy, capable, effective, reliable. A Scriptural example of this type of prosperity is found in the Old Testament book of Daniel, as Daniel and his three friends, Hananiah, Mishael and Azariah (also known as Shadrach, Meschach and Abednego), were found to excel above all the other king's men. Daniel himself is described as having "an excellent spirit."

God used these men, and their prosperity, to move the hearts of kings toward commanding their entire kingdoms to "...honor and worship the God of Daniel" (Daniel 6:26). We see in Acts, thousands of years later, that people from this land (the land of the Medes and Persians) are present at the day of Pentecost (Acts 2). This is evidence that the impact of these men's lives, and their influence in their culture for the glory of God, lasted throughout generations, for many centuries. So if evangelism, or "being the light of the world" and influencing culture, is important to you, then listen up! You and your children's children can experience God's prosperity and influence your culture for generations to come.

Every child begins changing into an adult at some point between the ages of ten to fourteen. Yes, most fourteen year olds can actually make a baby! The decade from age fifteen to twenty-five is truly a decade of emergence. These years are a time of

---

[1] Many would consider this a controversial statement due to the historical disenfranchisement of this people and centuries of persecution and discrimination against them. The Jewish culture and identity of Jewish people, however, have certainly persisted through well over three thousand years of history. In this sense, the identity of the Jew has thrived!

transition. Transition is difficult, awkward and uncomfortable for everyone. Rites of passage are not only helpful, but are in fact necessary and essential, for smooth and prosperous transitions. Without these ceremonies we as a people flounder at best.

A coming of age rite of passage ceremony can set a young man (age thirteen) and a young woman (age twelve) on course to thrive! A father and mother who skillfully and thoroughly plan for a special day of events to honor their teenager may be likened to a skilled archer who draws the bow and takes aim to prepare the arrow for hitting its target. Setting aside a single day for a significant event in recognition and celebration of your budding adult creates wholeness within his or her young adult heart.

Equally important is learning to seize every opportunity throughout these teenage years to affirm, recognize and celebrate your child's budding adulthood. This consistent affirmation breeds competence. I believe the series of rites of passages defined in this book for the junior high and high school years can empower your son and/or daughter to know who they are and what they have to offer early in life - before the age of eighteen.

One goal in parenting is to help a young adult son or daughter launch out into the world like an arrow, heading straight toward the bullseye of his or her life target. A rite of passage serves as the drawing back of the bow. It propels a new teenager into his or her own clear sense of identity and purpose. A rite of passage also empowers the parents in their own transition: letting go!

My sincere hope is that this book will inspire parents to celebrate and honor the passage of their children from childhood to adulthood with their own family tradition of rites of passage. The proliferation of such a tradition will lead to wiser teenagers, healthier families and an increase of godliness within our communities!

Thank you for believing that you can raise thriving teenagers. I pray peace and prosperity (wholeness and competence) upon you and your children. Glory to God in the highest, peace on earth and good will toward men! Shalom.

Chapter 1 – What is a Rite of Passage?

A quick Google search will lead you to Wikipedia's definition of a rite of passage - "a ritual event that marks a person's progress from one status to another. It is a universal phenomenon which can show anthropologists what social hierarchies, values and beliefs are important in specific cultures. Rites of passage are often ceremonies surrounding events such as other milestones within puberty, coming of age, marriage and death. Initiation ceremonies such as baptism, confirmation and Bar or Bat mitzvah are considered important rites of passage for persons of their respective religions."[2]

The Jewish people prevalently celebrate a coming of age rite of passage for their sons and daughters. The celebration for daughters, traditionally at age twelve, is called a Bat mitzvah, which is Hebrew for "daughter of the commandments." The celebration for sons is traditionally at age thirteen and is called a Bar mitzvah, which is Hebrew for "son of the commandments."

God gave His commandments to the Jewish people as the path to prosperity. "I have laid before you life and death. Choose

[2] http://en.wikipedia.org/wiki/Rite_of_passage

life" (Deuteronomy 30:19). Through His commandments God reveals the way of life that works. For those who obey His commandments and walk in His ways, life works well. (See the blessings in Deuteronomy 28:1-14, for example.) For those who disregard the commandments and follow their own way - life doesn't work well. (See the curses in the rest of that chapter, verses 15-68.)

In the New Testament, Jesus says, "I came that they might have life and have it more abundantly"(John 10:10). He also said that he "came to fulfill, not abolish, the law" (Matthew 5:17). These commandments, or ways of God, are still the path to prosperity. Jesus empowers His followers to walk in these ways of God, obeying His commands, by the power of the Holy Spirit dwelling within, so that we may truly have abundant life. He taught us to pray, "Your kingdom come. Your will be done on earth as it is in heaven" (Matthew 6:10). It is hard to imagine a heaven where God's commands are disregarded and life is broken!

The coming of age rite of passage is a recognition ceremony. It is a ritual intended to recognize the young man's and young woman's exit from childhood and entry into adulthood. The Bar/ Bat mitzvah draws a line in time for the honoree and for the parents and the attendees. It says, "We recognize you as an adult with us now, one who walks in God's ways with us." The ceremony also gives the honoree the opportunity to declare his/ her own choice for life: the choice to obey God and live abundantly -- to thrive and prosper.[3] This day of recognition ushers in a new level of accountability for the young adult honoree.

This day of recognition also draws a line in time for the parents and the faith community surrounding the family. The parents and the community will now recognize the honoree as a young adult in their midst: A young man! A young woman! This

---

[3] Please keep in mind my definition of "prosperity" - wholeness and competence, a clarity of identity combined with reliability and trustworthiness, discussed in more detail on page 25 in the Introduction.

is significant. Our culture tends to treat children as kids even into adulthood. (To this day, my father-in-law calls my wife and I "kids!") This rite of passage event settles within the hearts of parents and other adults in the community that this young man, this young woman, is no longer a child, but now is an adult member of the community.

Chapter 2 – An Invitation to Fathers!

Without the recognition that comes from a rite of passage, a young man or young woman is left to pursue recognition of their adulthood in their own misguided way. In the West, we live in a cultural epidemic of destructive rites of passage. In the absence of a healthy ceremony, the rites of passage that our youth seek may be pre-marital sex, gang membership, drunkenness, illegal drug experimentation, criminal activity, and countless other unhealthy means. The human psyche will not tolerate being ignored. We will be recognized as an adult, one way or another, even to our own detriment. Especially without a father's love and affirmation, in the words of Eddy Rabbit, we go "looking for love in all the wrong places, looking for love in too many faces."

Gordon Dalbey (*www.abbafather.com*), author of *Healing the Masculine Soul*, *Sons of the Father*, and *Fight Like a Man*, explains this father-wound perhaps as well as anyone. In one of his seminars I heard him recount the story of a nun who worked at a prison. One day, she said, a prisoner asked her to buy him a Mother's Day card for his mother. She did, and the word traveled like wildfire around the prison. Deluged with requests, she called Hallmark Cards, who obliged with huge boxes of Mother's Day cards as a donation. The warden arranged for each inmate to draw a number, and they lined up through the cell blocks to get their cards.

Weeks later, the nun was looking ahead on her calendar, and decided to call Hallmark again and ask for as many Father's Day cards, in order to avoid another rush. As Father's Day approached, the warden announced free cards were again available at the chapel. To the nun's surprise, *not a single prisoner* ever asked her for a Father's Day card.

Like Dalbey, I believe the "father-wound" is epidemic among us. The father-wound is most often a wound of emotional as well as physical absence. Therefore this book is a very direct invitation to fathers to "engage the blade."[4] If you have ever sat on a riding lawnmower and driven around the yard without "engaging the blade" you know how futile this can be. A father who overlooks or ignores the passage of his children into adulthood can be equally futile.

The father has the power either to prosper the soul of a teenager or to wound it. Biologically, it is the father who determines the gender of a child. The mother's egg has an "X" chromosome. The father's sperm has either an "X" or a "Y" chromosome. If the father's "X" fertilizes the egg, the child is a girl (XX). If the father's "Y" fertilizes the egg, the child is a boy (XY).[5]

Likewise, the father is the most influential determinate of the teenager's inner sense of wholeness and competence. The impact of his absence can be irrevocable. However, when the father is able to "engage the blade" by recognizing his teenage daughter or teenage son with a coming of age rite of passage ceremony, the gender identity and inner sense of wholeness and competence within his teenager will prosper!

---

[4] Frank Midgley is a former youth pastor and teacher who coined this term for me. It refers to the futility of riding through your yard on a riding lawnmower (living life) with a disengaged blade!

[5] Thanks to Dr. Omar Hamada for his help with these medical facts.

The coming of age rite of passage (such as the traditional Jewish Bar/Bat mitzvah) is truly one of God's ways in the earth today. It is an effective event to help our sons and daughters transition deliberately and prosperously into adulthood with a clear sense of wholeness and competence. A coming of age rite of passage also helps us as parents transition into our new adult-to-adult relationship with our children. A skilled archer knows what is required for a proper "release" to fire the arrow. In much the same way, parents must learn how to skillfully "let go" or "back off" for the teenagers to truly emerge as an adult heading for his/her life target!

I think most fathers do not feel especially influential with their teenagers, yet most fathers deeply want their teenagers to thrive. If you will begin to incorporate some of the rites of passage in this book in the life of your family, you will find a path to your teenager's heart, and you will be empowered to reveal your good intentions to your son/daughter.

In the movie, *It's Cloudy with a Chance of Meatballs*, there is a wonderful scene where the girl takes the monkey-thought-translator off of the monkey and puts it on the father. The teenager for the first time in his life is able to hear the true thoughts and feelings of love and affirmation from his father.

The series of rites of passage laid out in this book can have a similar result. I have personally witnessed the effect in my own family and many others.

Typically, throughout early childhood, most of the discipline, nurture and training delivered to a child comes through his/her mother or another female. When a child becomes a young adult, he/she may naturally have resentment toward Mom, simply because he/she feels "grown up" now. When Mom is correcting, this young adult may feel like he or she is being treated like a little boy or little girl. When a father addresses a teenager for instruction, correction, or discipline, the teenager may subconsciously respond better, because he/she feels "called up" by Dad.

Every child and every family is different. I recommend certain grade levels for celebrating your child's passage into adulthood in specific ways. Some families may choose to accelerate or delay the timetable. Some families may choose to combine several topics in one year or at one time. Allow these resources to serve as a guide to help you "draw the bow" so that, at the appropriate time, you can effectively "release" your young adult child to leave your home like an arrow shot toward the bullseye of his/her life target.

BONUS: *Sticks and stones may break my bones, but words can crush or build me!*

As a father, as a mother, you perhaps more than any other person have the ability to instill confidence and dignity within your child. You have an equal ability to reduce your child to a fractured and wounded person. Your spoken words may have much more power than you think. "There is life and death in the tongue" (Proverbs 18:21). The Jewish practice of a father praying to God and asking His blessings upon each child by name truly merits your consideration.[6]

The movie *What the Bleep Do We Know* is interesting. Among other things, it documents the results of a study on water molecules. Jars of water were placed in closets. On the outside of each closet door were different words like "Love," "Happiness," "Anger," "Resentment" -- one word to each closet. Students were then asked to stand in front of each closet door and think or imagine and feel only that particular word. Then the student was to enter the closet and look at the jar of water thinking, feeling, or speaking to the jar of water anything that conveyed this single word.

After several students had participated by "visiting" the jar of water with the message written on the outside of the closet door,

---

[6]This happens not just in the Bar/Bat mitzvah rites of passage ceremonies, but also during the weekly Shabbat meal (see the bonus chapter at the end of the book for more on this Friday evening tradition).

the water from each jar was examined under a microscope. The remarkable results revealed that the water molecules which came from jars in closets with a positive word were organized in symmetrical designs. The molecular structure of the water that was "blessed" with positive thoughts, feelings and words appeared ordered, integrated, attractive, and healthy looking. The water molecules from jars in the closets with a negative word looked chaotic, mangled, and ugly. The molecular structure of the water which had been bombarded with negative thoughts, feelings, and words appeared deranged, scattered and fractured. The movie points out that the human body is comprised of approximately 70% water! This points toward scientific evidence that positive words, thoughts, and feelings bless (help) us and negative words, thoughts, and feelings curse (harm) us on a molecular level!

There are many different ways to bless your children. One simple, yet profound way is with the spoken word.

Chapter 3 – Why Rites of Passage?

The most compelling perspective I have read for having a coming of age rite of passage ceremony comes from Craig Hill (*www.familyfoundations.com*) in his books *Bar Barakah* and *Ancient Paths*. His *Ancient Paths* seminars and these two books are especially helpful for parents with troubled teens, and/or for families with intense conflicts between parents and teenagers. I highly recommend Craig Hill's books and seminar events. Much of this chapter is greatly influenced by his work.

If you have been married for a year or more, you may have felt at times like you wish your weren't married or wondered if this was really a good idea after all. We all go through low points and times of doubt. I imagine, however, that you have always been certain, since your wedding day, that you indeed are married!

If you are married, have you ever doubted the fact that you are married? Since you have been married, has there ever been a time when you thought, "I wonder if I am really married or not?" (At this point you may be laughing or slightly confused, wondering, "What?") Please ask yourself, "Why is this?" "Why have I never doubted the fact that I am indeed married?"

Perhaps, like me, you had a day where your family and friends all gathered together. You wore a unique suit, tuxedo, or dress. There was a ceremony with music, vows, readings, and several witnesses. People dressed up! Some folks traveled from afar and at great expense to themselves to attend. There were flowers, pictures, bird seed, gifts, cards, etc. You may have had a large party after the ceremony – a celebration with food, drink, more music, friends, laughter, gifts and lots of fun. A wedding is a rite of passage ceremony and celebration.

One of the culminating effects of the wedding day ceremony and celebration is that it creates a certainty within our hearts and minds that we are definitely married now. It is a rite of passage out of *singleness* into *marriage*. The wedding also creates a certainty within the hearts and minds of our family, friends, acquaintances, and the general public that we are definitely married now. The wedding has changed something on the inside of you and also on the inside of others that once and for all settles the issue. No more question mark!

Now, compare this certainty to how you felt as a child changing into an adult. Do you remember being eighteen years old, going to a new place for the first time and feeling like a "little girl inside" or a "little boy inside?" Do you remember beginning a new job, or going to a school parent meeting for one of your children, or going to traffic court and feeling like a "little girl" or "little boy" inside? Perhaps you still felt this at the age of thirty, forty, or even fifty.

Some of us adults feel like a child on the inside, even into old age! This feeling seems to never go away for some. Others have stories about when they remember being "called up" or recognized in some way as now being "one of the men" or now being "one of the women," but still wondering at times, "Am I really a man?" or "Am I really a woman?"

The reality is that, in our western culture, the feeling of truly being an adult remains ambiguous for many. It is not clear. Certain events or moments in life have a way of amplifying this "question mark." My guess is that if you feel this way, you probably did not have a rite of passage ceremony celebrating your passage from childhood into adulthood.

Living life with this unresolved "question" inside ends up undermining your ability to be present. Living with this question mark on the inside causes you to withdraw, or keep quiet, or sometimes not even show up in a conversation, in a meeting, or in a relationship. You discount yourself. You dismiss ideas, thoughts, and opinions that come up in your mind, that come from your heart.

This "inner question mark" can also create a discontentedness, which can then drive you toward unhealthy pursuits in misguided efforts to fill the void. If you are not able to be fully present in life, then you end up having a long list of regrets, resentments, losses, missed opportunities, frustrations and disappointments, which you have brought upon yourself by listening to and feeding this "inner question mark."

The ability to live fully present is vitally important. It is important for you, your spouse, your children, your family and friends, who all want and need you to be present, more than anything. God created you to be a blessing, and Jesus has paid the price to remove everything that hinders you! (If you feel hindered in life and long to be more effective in relationships, work, or any area of your life, I highly recommend attending an Ancient Paths Seminar, *www.familyfoundations.com*, a Landmark Forum, *w w w . l a n d m a r k e d u c a t i o n . c o m*, or an Encounter, *www.fullyaliveministries.org*).

A rite of passage blessing ceremony and celebration has the potential to change something on the inside of us. It can once and for all settle the issue of whether or not "I am a man" or "I am a woman." If you have ever wondered, "What is a real man?," and you were born male, then go look in the mirror. If you wonder what a real woman looks like, and you were born female, then go look in the mirror. However, if you want to settle once and for all in your heart and mind the fact that you are no longer "a little girl" or "a little boy," then plan yourself a rite of passage ceremony celebration. Invite your friends, your supportive family members and your mentor, or counselor, or pastor, and have a rite of passage celebration of your adulthood!

Now consider the example of God the Father with Jesus. In his book, *Bar Barakah*, Craig Hill teaches the context of the event that happened at Jesus' baptism by John the Baptist (see Matthew 3). It was a tradition in that culture, at the appropriate time, for the father to bring his adult son before the town elders at the city gate. He would present his son to the elders of the city and say "This is my son, in whom I am well pleased." This would be the day that the father would begin his succession plan for the family business, and the son would become his successor. It was the father's way of saying, in essence, "You have known me and my work all these years. You have conducted business with me. Now, this is my son. He will carry on the family business. I place my full trust and confidence in him, and I ask you to do the same. My son will now carry on my work!"

Do you hear it? The father is saying, "This is my son, in whom I am well pleased."

I ask you to imagine something for a moment. Put yourself in Jesus' shoes. Imagine that you are led by the Spirit one day to go to your cousin, John the Baptist, who is preaching and baptizing in the wilderness in the Jordan River. Today, you are going to make yourself known publicly and be baptized by him. As you approach, you may have some feelings of trepidation. You think you know who you are inside, but you are not sure how people around you are going to take it and so you are a little uncertain. "What will people think?"

Perhaps you even want to be incognito or slightly invisible. Isn't it natural, at times, to want to remain discreet? However, Cousin John sees you coming and says, "Behold, the Lamb of God who takes away the sins of the world!" In that annoying booming voice, he is calling you out! "The One, whose sandals I am not worthy to untie!" (Busted! Now you are cringing on the inside, really wondering what people will think, and why he won't just shut up already!)

Now, all eyes are on you. You walk into the water and after a slight argument with your cousin John, he baptizes you. Perhaps people are wondering, "What is happening here? We know this guy -- who does he think he is?" You are wondering, "How do I explain this?" "What do I say?"

You are a little nervous, that is, until the Spirit comes down on top of you in the form of a dove for all to see; and the Father speaks! From the clouds, you and everyone around you hear this amazing, thunderous voice: "This is my Son, in whom I am well pleased!" AAHHHHHH. Way to go, Dad! Thank you, my Father in heaven! That settles it! Now, I know for certain, that who I feel like I am on the inside is real. No more question mark! Now everyone knows. There is a certainty with no more explanation required.

I think puberty has a lot in common with this moment. A young woman can feel awkward about her developing body. Perhaps she feels more self-conscious than ever before. Her father may also feel awkward. This little girl he used to tickle and wrestle is now a curvy young woman, and she still wants to sit on his lap and be held close.

If the Dad withdraws at this time, he can unintentionally send her a message of rejection, which increases her sense of awkwardness and embarrassment. Her insecurity may result in her looking for love, affection and recognition in "all the wrong places and too many faces." A young man can feel awkward about his voice changing and the fact that he has an erection at the oddest times. The rite of passage ceremony and the guided conversations outlined in this book can have the same effect for your teenager that I believe God's voice from heaven had on Jesus that day.

Like Craig Hill, I believe that the day Jesus was baptized by John and that God spoke from heaven was like a rite of passage for Jesus. It had a dramatic effect inside his heart and mind, and in the hearts and minds of those around Jesus. Another day similar to this one was the day of Jesus' transfiguration before His closest disciples. God provided these moments for Jesus' sake and for the sake of those around Him (as well as for ours!). They settled something inside of him, and inside of everyone else around him.

These events in Jesus' life certainly illustrate what the rite of passage ceremony and celebration is all about. The life Jesus lived and the death he died definitely required Him to be present and have certainty within Himself. He needed clarity about His identity and his purpose -- no room for question marks! God knew this and He settled it for His Son, in front of everyone. Jesus lived a life which exemplifies wholeness and competence. You as a father, you as a mother, have the very unique and special ability to settle something on the inside of your sons' and your daughters' hearts and minds – their manhood and womanhood.

My Personal Journey

I can remember my first day of junior high like it was yesterday. New seventh graders filled the bleachers. The principal had us all come into the gymnasium. He stood at center court and made some not-so-welcoming announcements through a harsh, echo-ey sound system from a microphone with a single stand. Then each teacher came to the microphone and called a list of names. Their students were required to form a shoulder to shoulder line in the middle of the gym floor, facing the gawking crowd, waiting until the class was complete. Then in a single file line they would follow the teachers out of the "arena" to their classrooms.

My buddies and I pointed and laughed at the awkwardness of some of the people called forth. When a student tripped or dropped something, trying to carry too much, the gymnasium would roar with laughter. It was awful. Fear and anxiety caused my heart to fill my throat. Then the horrible happened. My name was called. I remember wishing I could totally disappear. I was filled with insecurity, self-consciousness, and fear. I can honestly say the worst two years of my life were my seventh and eighth grade years.

I had a tiny moral compass which was quickly overwhelmed by a sea of doubt and insecurity within me. I was unprepared for what was happening inside of me and around me. The choices I made to compensate for these insecurities became regretful and spiraled me into worse choices. Halfway through my eighth grade year, my best friend, Adam Swanson, and his praying mother, Flo Swanson, finally persuaded me to become "born again." The night I knelt on my bedroom floor, in between phone calls with Adam and his mother, and asked Jesus to fill me, was the turning of the tide.

The presence of God came into my room, into my heart, and filled me with a life changing peace. My soul flooded with a warm sensation of acceptance. What a relief! No more striving. I was okay. The God of the universe, Creator of all things, loved me and welcomed me, just as I am. That was the beginning of a long journey to become fully integrated within myself and at peace with God in every area of my life. It was around the age of thirty-five that I fully settled in to feeling comfortable within my own skin, living a life with rare regrets. Thank God, He is faithful to finish what he starts!

Bill Ligon (*www.thefathersblessing.com*) held a weekend of meetings in my church in March, 1997. I was nearing my thirtieth birthday, and still felt very much like a little boy on the inside. However, this weekend event had a tremendous impact on me. So, I invited my friends and family to celebrate my thirtieth birthday with my own rite of passage ceremony!

Close friends, my pastor, my parents and in-laws were there. To some, I had to explain it. Others, knew what I meant. I basically asked every person to come to my thirtieth birthday party with a present. The present I wanted was a spoken and/or written blessing to be read to me at the party. It was a very memorable event.

Some people read to me passages of Scripture, some read poems, one wrote a song just for me and sang it. Others simply gave me a card with their favorite word of encouragement to me. Some prayed over me. Some gave me gifts that had a purpose, as a token of their blessing to me. All in all, that day, I received many, many affirmations of my manhood, and my value as a husband, father, son, and friend. It was significant. I enjoyed it so much that I actually repeated it for myself in two other future events. Yes, I had a three-peat. This was healing to my heart. And my heart needed healing!

These blessing ceremonies and celebrations, which I planned for myself, settled something on the inside of me. Since then, I have lived my life much more present and much more faithfully engaged. Because of this fullness, when my two oldest daughters became young women, I was prepared to truly bless them. Out of my fullness I was able to impart a powerful experience of recognition and acknowledgement of their womanhood. The result is glorious. The teenage years in my home are wonderful years. My young adult daughters are delightful, remarkable people. And they are the light of the world in every place they find themselves.

You can only give what you have. You cannot give what you do not have. The purpose of a rite of passage blessing ceremony and celebration for your son or daughter is to settle within his or her heart and mind the reality that childhood has ended and adulthood has begun, to begin to establish their identity as a man or a woman. To be able to do that, the first step in preparing to bless him or her is to make sure that you have first received this blessing in your own life.

It doesn't have to take thirty-five years! I believe the first day of seventh grade can be a good day; a day in which a young man or young woman can feel confident and purposeful. Parents have what it takes to make the difference, especially fathers. And if you don't have what it takes, you can get it. Like me, you can plan a rite of passage ceremony and celebration for yourself and for your spouse.

I strongly recommend you hold these types of events individually for one person at a time. Once you are blessed, then you can plan one for your son and/or daughter. You can empower your young adult to be at rest and confident in his or her value and purpose in life early in their teenage years! And no matter how old you are, as long as you are alive, it is never too late!

Chapter 4 – Preparing for the Rite of Passage (Fifth – Seventh Grade, Ages 11-13)

Winston Churchill, like many, denounced Christianity as "childish" after his first year of college. He rejected the Christian faith of his childhood nanny, until he became a prisoner of war! When he was taken captive in India as a young journalist on the front lines of the British-Indian war, he wrote in his journal, "Empty atheistic philosophies are for rich, comfortable people." Indeed, "there are no atheists in the foxhole!" I don't believe it to be coincidence that Sir Winston never received his father's affirmation.

The affirmation of a father, through a rite of passage ceremony, empowers a young man or young woman to take for themselves the faith of their parents and become an internally grounded person, not swayed so easily by external forces (i.e. peer pressure or non-believing college professors!). Yet, the event itself is meaningless without proper preparation.

This chapter is intended to help you prepare yourself and your budding young adult for this coming of age event and for walking in a new relationship after the event. The event is intended to be a threshold.   Once you pass through it, you hope your son/ daughter enters into a new understanding of himself/herself. You also hope you enter into new territory in walking with your son/ daughter in a consultant-type relationship -- releasing him/her to increasing maturity and independence from you!

Some will say that it is impossible to treat teenagers in our culture as adults and truly give them independence and responsibilities. I say that belief is the very reason that so many twenty, thirty and forty year olds wonder who they are and wander in purposelessness. Let's put an end to this wandering. Let's bring the value, identity and usefulness in the world of our sons and daughters into focus and clarity early in life, before they leave home, before the age of eighteen!

How do you back off to give them room to experience their own consequences for their own choices? What responsibilities can you give them? What preparations can you make for this transfer of responsibility? How can you allow them to experience their own crises? What can you do to help them truly discover their own personal "God-shaped vacuum?"

This chapter teaches you how you can give them responsibilities early in their young teenage years, while living at home, so they can become equipped with decision making skills and independence before they leave home. I hope you will use these suggestions, and create others, to find ways to nurture their competence by truly relying on them. May God equip you to skillfully prepare them to enter their adulthood and effectively release them to fly!

Plan a Meeting Place

What is the love language of your child? What is his or her favorite activity? Or restaurant? Or park? I recommend you plan for a series of "meetings" that involve fun and entertainment as well as time to chat – face to face together with father and mother (when possible) that are uniquely catered to your rising fifth or sixth grader.

Commit to a succession of scheduled times together (for example, every Saturday morning for the next six weeks). Take a hike, go to a park, eat out, get coffee or smoothies. Any combination of fun activities and good food sets the stage for conversations in which you introduce these key topics:

1. Prepare for Changes
2. Get Grounded
3. Choose Wisely
4. Know the Hebrew Scriptures – the Culture of God

I recommend separate times for each topic to keep it simple and focused. Having talks in the same special place each time also helps keep focus and creates anticipation. Allow time between meetings (one to four weeks) to provide time for your rising fifth or sixth grader to think it all over and hopefully participate more and more in each successive meeting. You will find that each meeting triggers a beneficial sense of anticipation for the next meeting.

One good idea is to announce on the eleventh birthday, that "you are almost a young man/woman now. I want to meet with you on the first Saturday morning for these next four months to begin preparing for your rite of passage/blessing ceremony, when we celebrate you becoming a man/woman!"

Now, let's walk through each of these topics. Here are some guidelines as to what to cover as you prepare your son/daughter for adulthood.

Prepare for Changes

Puberty brings on changes!

1. Girls/Boys seem to "lose their cooties" in the sixth grade. Attraction arrives!
2. Bodies change. Hair grows. Body odor thrives. Voices change. Babies can now be made.

3. Emotions change. Hormone cycles cause new mood swings. Passions intensify (anger, lust, etc.).
4. Peer interests and conversations change. They talk about topics never discussed before. Peers talk about each other differently.
5. Expectations change. Children ask parents for money -- young adults work to earn money! Children have to be reminded to do things -- young adults make notes and take efforts to remind themselves.

In your first meeting with your son or daughter show them a copy of this list, or create your own list of changes. Talk about them. List all of these changes in conversation with them and assure them that these changes are all good! You might say something like this:

"God has set a biological alarm clock that goes off at this age to change us (all humans!) from being a child to becoming an adult. This is a time in your life that God has planned, and looked forward to for a long time. Childhood comes to an end and adulthood begins."

Point out that this happens to everyone (not just them!). Let them know you and your spouse went through these changes (their mother and their father went through these changes). Tell them how you felt during adolescence. Transition is happening and it is good! It is normal!

Ask them if they have noticed this already about themselves. What changes do they see among their peers? Assure them that at times these changes will seem good and exciting, and at other times they can be embarrassing or stressful. You might say something along these lines:

"There will be times you feel happy about becoming a young woman/man; and other times that you wish you could just remain a child. This mixture of emotions is normal too!"

Prepare them for these mood swings. These mixed emotions are part of every transition in life. Your son/daughter needs to hear you talk about these things. When you tell them about something they have already begun to experience (or soon will be experiencing), it comforts them and reassures them that they are normal. Nearly everyone feels "odd" or "weird" during a transition. Most teens feel overly self-conscious and "weird" or "odd" about the very normal changes they are noticing within themselves. You have the special ability and privilege to comfort your son/daughter by simply letting them know that you are familiar with these changes.

At times they will want more responsibility and more independence; at other times they will want everything done for them and just to play (revert to childhood). Rarely does anyone enjoy going through change. The transition of going from childhood to adulthood happens over a period of six to ten years! Because all of this is new, it can feel awkward, but it is normal. Tell them how you felt during adolescence.

Just hearing that you felt this way too, and learning that they are not alone in these feelings and changes, can bring tremendous relief, comfort and peace. This shared knowledge can build a bridge of trust between you and your teenager.

There will come a time when these changes have finished, and adulthood fully sets in. Assure them that this transition will come to an end. Point out to them that every person is different and on a slightly different time table. Encourage them to be empathetic to their peers. Here's an example of a way to say this:

> "These changes are new to you now, but pretty soon they just seem normal. Have you noticed your friends changing too? Do you know anyone who seems to be changing sooner than most people? Do you know anyone who seems to still be more like a little child? How do you think they feel about themselves? What do you think you can do to help him/her? I just want you to know that I am proud of you, and I notice that you are going through

these changes (or you are getting ready to start having these changes yourself!)."

These types of conversations can help them be less self-centered, which is critical to their confidence level. End this conversation by thanking them for spending this time with you and affirming what you see in them that you enjoy and admire, with something like this:

"I realize even talking about some of these things can be uncomfortable. Thank you for having this conversation with me and letting us spend this time together. I am impressed by you. You are ... *(identify positive traits here to affirm your son/daughter).*
"And I want you to know that I have experienced these very same things that you and your friends are beginning to experience. I am here for you."

In closing, pray together, giving thanks for your son/daughter. Thank God for bringing them through their childhood to this moment of change. Thank God for His design in bringing about all these changes at this time in their life.

After this meeting, I recommend you go straight home and write them a letter before going to bed that same night.[7] In the letter, reminisce about their childhood and some of your favorite memories and thoughts of them when they were little. Be vulnerable and transparent with them about your feelings and trepidations about them growing up. I remember wanting to cry at times, realizing that I was losing my little girl to her own adulthood. Write in your letter what you noticed about their posture, their eye contact, their insights, during your conversation, which demonstrated to you their maturity and readiness for this season of their life.

---

[7] See Appendix C, One Dad's Letter to his Thirteen Year Old Son

Affirm them and tell them you recognize their strengths and talents. Tell them you love them and you are very pleased with them. Give this letter to them within the next twenty-four to forty-eight hours after your meeting. The intention is to further reinforce to them your confidence in them and the significance of this time of change in their life. What a young adolescent needs most when they are beginning to go through puberty is this type of positive recognition and affirmation of these changes they are experiencing.

Note for parents of a daughter - Ideally, Mom or a close adult female friend should talk in detail with young women about what to expect for their first menstrual cycle in a separate conversation. However, Dad needs to let his daughter know that he is aware of this change that will occur in her and excited about this for her. She will now carry the potential every month for bringing a new person into the world. Dad needs to affirm her in this unique ability. This is a blessing, not a curse. God created her this way and it is good. He has determined this time for her to begin ovulating. He has confidence in her.

Come into agreement with Him by telling her that you are proud of her and look forward to the day she receives her first menstrual cycle. This will be a day and an event to celebrate together. Words of encouragement and affirmation are critical -- especially from Dad -- throughout adolescence.

Get Grounded

Now it is time for them to begin taking responsibility for their own study of the Bible, their own attendance of church, their own prayer life and journal, their own times of solitude with God. For example: They can set their own alarm to wake up in time to prepare to attend church. (If they sleep late, perhaps by age thirteen they can be left behind – experiencing consequences for poor choices). They can lead a family devotional from their own Bible. They can keep a prayer journal and report to the family their own answers to prayer. They can keep their own solitude times with God. This is the time for your son/daughter to mature spiritually as well as physically and emotionally.

It is also an important time to learn financial responsibility. A fifth or sixth grader can work to earn money through chores within the home and for extended family, friends, and neighbors -- doing the laundry, dishes, floors, yard mowing, filing bills/papers, washing cars, babysitting, etc.

This will help them earn their own money to prepare for the seventh grade when they can buy their own back-to-school supplies and clothes, or purchase their own school lunches, field trips or gifts for friends' birthdays with the money they have earned. Ask yourself, what measures you can take as a parent to help your rising sixth grader begin to live his or her own life independently within your home by the time they begin high school. This will help them to begin learning financial independence, prepared for when they leave home one day.

My mother was in the habit of buying my blue jeans at the flea market (this is not a joke!). At the end of sixth grade, I put my foot down and boldly announced to her that I was not going to be wearing any "flea market blue jeans" to the seventh grade. She said, "No problem, when it comes time to buy your back to school clothes next year, I will give you the same amount of money I would spend at the flea market, and you can buy whatever jeans you want." Great hand-off Mom! She totally put the ball in my court and made it my problem, not hers.

Fortunately, my father allowed me to use the family lawn mower all summer to cut grass for neighbors. I worked hard and saved my money. When the seventh grade started, I wore Levi's jeans and Izod shirts. I have not worn flea market clothes since!

Give your son/daughter as much independence and personal responsibility and freedom as soon as possible. Here are some recommendations for how to begin:

1. Help him/her develop a habit of daily Bible reading using Proverbs. Buy them a new Bible and present it as a special gift. Explain your desire for them to begin caring for their own soul and pursuing their own

personal growth and education of God's ways. Show them a calendar with thirty-thirty one days in a month and the book of Proverbs with thirty one chapters. Invite them to read a Proverb a day (on the first of the month you can start with Proverbs 1, on the tenth of the month, start with Proverbs 10, etc.). As much as you are available, read this together every day for the first month (pick a specific time of day -- bedtime, or breakfast, or dinner time). When reading together, allow for time to talk about what certain verses mean. Answer their questions. Ask them to tell you their understanding of certain verses. Discuss this around the dinner table throughout the week.

2. Help him/her learn how to pray. When I spent the night with my grandfather as a young child, at bedtime he would invite me into his room to kneel beside him. He told me this is where he prays every night. He would first thank God for all the blessings of the day. Then he would tell me to do the same. Then he would ask God to help everyone who needs help: "Lord heal Sarah from cancer, Lord help Joe get a job, Lord comfort Mary for the loss of her husband, Lord help Mike work out his problems with his employees, etc." At bedtime is the perfect time to give thanks for the blessings of the day, and to ask for God's help for troubles (your own and those of others!) Pray out-loud together. Lead your son/daughter by example.

3. Buy him/her a new watch and/or alarm clock. Explain your desire to see him/her to grow in personal responsibility for attending school and church on time. Throughout the next week and Sunday, leave it to him/her to wake up, shower, dress, come to breakfast, etc., on his/her own. See how they do. Allow them to experience their own consequences for oversleeping, or missing breakfast, or not having clean clothes, etc.

4. Give a journal. Explain your desire to see him/her grow in keeping a record of prayers to God -- thanksgivings

and requests, as well as keeping a record of events, of blessings and troubles. Invite him/her to share something from his/her journal with you once a month to help develop the habit. Do not require full disclosure. Allow your son/daughter to choose the entries they share with you. Respect their privacy. Affirm his/her dignity and independence.

5. Go to a bank together. Help your son/daughter open a checking account. At home, Give him/her a "job description" and a "salary." Give him/her a list of "bills" – things they will need to be prepared to pay for themselves. Include tithing (to the church) and taxes (to you/house budget), school lunches, sports fees, dance lesson dues, movie money, etc. Delegate the responsibility for these chores and expenses to them and hold them accountable. There are usually complaints at first. Remember the words of Scott Peck from *The Road Less Travelled*: "Life is hard, but once you realize that, then it's not so bad."

All of these are ways to begin preparing your son/daughter for their coming of age rite of passage event. Whether you complete these over a six month period of time or two years, it doesn't matter. What is important is that you are spending time with your son/daughter, teaching, training and introducing the adult-world to them. These are valuable "deposits" you are making in their heart of love, affirmation, recognition and blessing.

Two of my children had a third grade teacher, Mrs. Jones, from New York. I affectionately call her "Mrs. Ellis Island." She is a firm believer in the third grader's ability to take responsibility for themselves, doing their own laundry, picking out their own clothes, remembering their books and assignments, etc. She strongly discourages parents from bringing anything to school that their child forgot to bring that day. She says, "if you always cover for them, then when will they learn to take care of it themselves!" She admonishes parents in the third grade orientation night at the beginning of the year, "Let them suffer through it."

So, with our third graders, we comfort them, tell them they will survive and encourage them to negotiate with their teacher or coach to work it out. Most importantly do not interfere and do not condemn them with *"why didn't you's"* or *"you should'ves."* Don't *"should"* on them! If you speak anything to them, speak words of praise and affirmation. Remind them that they are a good student and that everyone forgets things sometimes. You will empower them by what you say. You could cripple them by intervening and "protecting" them from having any loss or pain for their failure to deliver. You may also cripple them by condemning or criticizing them. Play the role of encourager and call them forth. It is time for them to "cowboy/cowgirl UP!"

Most transitions (maybe every one!) a person goes through are unsettling and move us out of our comfort zone. Adolescence is no exception. A natural tendency under stress or discomfort is to look for something outside of us to comfort: the acceptance of friends, a favorite movie or TV show, food, music, etc. Encourage your son/daughter to turn toward God during times of stress.

Jesus met the Samaritan woman at the well. She had looked to men to fill her neediness. He promised her a fountain within her to satisfy her thirst. In Revelation 3:20, Jesus invites Himself into the heart of anyone who will open: "I stand at the door and knock.... I will dine with him...." Jesus told His disciples "The Kingdom of God is within you." Paul refers to our body as "the temple of the Holy Spirit." God told the Israelites that He "would write (His) laws on their hearts." These examples demonstrate where true and lasting wholeness, well being, and refreshment come from: God with us, Emmanuel.

Train your son/daughter to call upon God and to notice His Presence within his/her own heart. This is integration, integrity, wholeness, etc. – fellowshipping with God inside of your own heart; welcoming His Presence to come and "dine" with you. This is learning to be internally grounded and secure; not looking to things or people outside of us; but looking to Him, who has come to live inside of you!

You want to nurture a change, from living life ruled by external influences, to being led internally. You are preparing your child for self-government and for the transfer to themselves of the responsibility for the wellness of their own soul and their personal relationship with God.

Don't Have A Problem with Having A Problem

Too often I think we adults (myself included!) have a problem with having a problem. For example, if my son forgets to do his homework until we are in the car on the way to school in the morning, this is a problem. If I shame him, or yell at him for having this problem, then I have a problem with having a problem. My son can fix the problem of forgotten homework. He cannot fix the problem of my condemnation.

I remember, in my first year of marriage, the first time I could not pay my rent on time. I freaked out. I did not know what to do. I had a problem: I couldn't pay my rent. But I also had an intense feeling of shame, guilt and fear. Should I commit suicide? The embarrassment I felt about having this problem paralyzed me. It turned a mole hill into a mountain. In this mindset, do you think I was capable of going out and creating some cash flow to solve my problem? No. Once I called my landlord, I was relieved. He did not yell at me or condemn me for this problem. He asked me some questions. He offered some alternatives. We worked out a solution.

A problem can always be solved with some effort. My son can tell his teacher he forgot his homework and ask for options. However, my son cannot handle me yelling or shaming him. So, allow your children to experience consequences (have problems) with your full support! When they fail, remind them that you believe in them. Tell your son/daughter that you know he/she doesn't make this mistake often. Assure your son/daughter that he/she can work through it and solve the problem. This empowers your child to succeed. This leads your child into internal groundedness. We tend to want to rescue our kids, but we need to resist this tendency.

Choose Wisely

Learning to choose wisely is one of life's greatest tasks. The ability to choose wisely is a learned skill. Parents have the greatest position of influence to impart wisdom. You can truly partner with your son or daughter to help him or her learn how to make good choices.

Children learn primarily through observation. So, evaluate how you make choices. Which of your decisions can you allow your budding teenager to witness up-close and personal? Begin training your son or daughter by sharing with him or her some of your dilemmas and choices that you must make. Let them see the steps you go through in determining your direction. Ask what he or she would choose if this were his or her decision. Discuss it. Explain to them why you make the choice you make. Here are some ways to give your son or daughter a "front row seat" to your decision:

1. Discuss it around the dinner table with your spouse. Pick an appropriate issue and let your child hear you talk it through together.
2. There is wisdom in a multitude of counselors (Proverbs 11:14). Do you seek counsel? Who do you get advice from when making a decision? Introduce your advisors to your son/daughter. Go to lunch together – your advisor, your son/daughter, and you. For as long as they were alive, my parents blessed me as the sun sank below the horizon each Friday evening. Since they were born I have done the same for my children. Another link in the chain of blessing that God imparted to Abraham. This book could enrich your family life for generations as it makes you part of an

eternal chain. ~ Rabbi Daniel Lapin, President American Alliance of Jews and Christians about the issue. Ask your son/daughter to be an engaged observer. Ask your advisor to tell your son/daughter how he/she sees it and why. Tell your son/daughter who you talk to for wise input and why!

3. Man shall not live by bread alone, but by every word that proceeds from the mouth of God (Deuteronomy 8:3). Find Scriptures you can read together that offer advice to you for this particular situation.

4. Pray out loud with them. Let them hear your prayers for wisdom and help in making decisions.

5. Listen for God to speak. Do you ever wait in stillness or quietness in prayer before God to listen in His presence? Perhaps you go for walks in solitude, or sit by the ocean, or watch the sun set. If so, then invite your son/daughter to do this with you in silence. Teach them to "tune in to God" by observing you waiting before Him in stillness.

6. Fast. If you fast, teach them how you fast, and why you fast. Invite them to join you. A total fast is not recommended for younger teenagers who are still growing. After their bodies mature, fasting is something they can more fully participate in.

7. Evaluate pros and cons. Divide a piece of paper into two parts and write down the list of advantages and disadvantages side by side. Show them how you do this.

8. Who else is affected by this choice? Make a list of the people impacted by this choice. Ask your son/daughter to help you come up with the list. Talk with him/her about how each person is affected.

9. Picture the possible end result. What are the possible outcomes? What outcomes seem most likely? What is the worst possible result of this choice? The best?

10. Live with your decision for a period of time before acting on it. Sometimes people say, "let me sleep on that." Making a decision and keeping it to yourself for a few

days or if possible, for a few weeks, can often be very helpful in making a better decision.

All of these are steps that can be taken to help you make wise choices. After you have introduced these to your son or daughter and shown them how you follow these steps in your own life with certain decisions, ask them to make a decision for themselves using some or all of these steps. After walking with them through these steps a few times, then let them do these things on their own. This process will help you make the transition to serve as a consultant, rather than a dictator, in your child's life.

Introduce the Hebrew Scriptures

The Hebrew Scriptures, known as the Old Testament, are often treated collectively as a "second class citizen" by many Christians in their reading and study of the Bible. However, it is in these Hebrew Scriptures, particularly the first five books of the Bible, known as "The Torah," where we find God's specific instructions for living. I like to think of the Hebrew Scriptures as the place where we learn the culture of God, the mind of God, the ways of God. His ways are the ways that work in the earth. Learning, studying and walking in God's ways help our marriages to work, help our careers and businesses to succeed, and help our children to prosper. Good results and blessings come from knowing His ways and following them.

Read this section to your son or daughter as a way to introduce them to the first five books of the Bible (Genesis, Exodus, Numbers, Leviticus, Deuteronomy).

Think of the nation of Israel as a baby firmly planted within the fertile womb of Egypt (Genesis 47:5, 6). Before they went to Egypt in the days of Joseph, they are a family of seventy people, an embryo nation (Genesis 46:26, 27). After living in Egypt for just over 400 years (Exodus 12:40, 41), they emerged as a baby nation of over one million people (Exodus 12:37). God caused His newly conceived nation Israel to grow for approximately forty decades (similar to a woman's forty week pregnancy) in the womb of Egypt (Genesis 50:22-26, Exodus 12:40, 41). In Egypt they were protected from outside enemies. They were provided with food. At some point they became slaves. During their slavery, they had no choices. They were told what to do, when to do it, yet they still had food "on tap." (They later complain in the wilderness about wanting to go back to Egypt where they were slaves and where they always had meat to eat!)

Finally, there comes a day of deliverance! (We refer to birth, as a delivery.) The plagues could be compared to contractions and the red sea as the breaking of the water (Exodus 4-15). The forty years in the wilderness are the baby nation's childhood. God "nurses them" with manna from heaven and quail from the wind (Exodus 16), water from rocks (Exodus 17), then gradually weans them from total daily reliance upon Him (Exodus 23:20-33). He leads them into a land where they can survive on their own work -- the Promised Land where they eat food from the land's produce, which would require their cultivation and work. The crossing of the Jordan is like their national Bar mitzvah (Joshua 1-3) . For the first time in forty years, once they cross the Jordan, they eat food from the produce of the land, and the manna from heaven stops (Joshua 5:10-12). (This is a great story, you really must read this!) The conquering of their promised land is like their teenaged years - their "emerging decade." They are required to be fully present and make their presence known in a radical way.

When you read the book of Exodus and the rest of the Torah from this perspective it helps to see how their experiences apply directly to our own journey toward maturity and independence. They became a very prosperous nation when they followed their loving Father's commands.

I think it is helpful to view God's laws as wise instructions from a loving Father who wants to benefit His children. When the Israelite people were slaves to Egypt they had no choices over their lives. Like little children, they were told what to do every day, when to eat, when to wake, when to sleep, where to live, etc. Once God freed them from Egypt, for the first time in several generations, they were going to have choices. They would be free! But this new freedom would require self-government.

This is similar to going from childhood (being told what to do and how to and when to, etc.) to adulthood (being free to make your own choices). God's laws helped them to mature into self-government. It was God's desire for them to live well and perpetuate their freedom. He wanted to see them prosper as an independent nation. Just like it is the parent's desire to help a teenager grow and become independent and prosperous as an adult. Therefore read Exodus together with your teenager in light of this journey from birth to childhood to adulthood. Life works well when we walk in God's ways. Adulthood requires courage. Notice God's word to Joshua -- "Be strong and courageous" (Joshua 1:1-9).

I hope this understanding of God as a loving Father, and His commands as wise guidance intended to prosper His children (natural born and adopted!), helps endear the Scriptures to you and to your son/daughter. Knowing and obeying the laws of God is what helps us to experience the abundant Life Jesus came to give us here and now, i.e. "Your Kingdom come, Your will be done on earth as it is in Heaven!" Remaining ignorant of His commands or disobeying them results in grief, pain, and loss. It is like ignoring gravity: It doesn't work out too well.

Therefore, this sixth grade year is a critical time to teach your child God's commands, which empower him/her to choose wisely. Perhaps more important than the commands themselves is teaching them to love reading and learning God's word. These stories can come alive for you and them. Cultivating a hunger for God and helping them love His written Word is one of the parent's greatest mandates. However, it is important to be beside (not above) your rising sixth grader during this time of learning. It is important to lead them by example and invite them to join you, rather than merely verbally commanding them. This can be the most difficult job of a parent -- to lead by example rather than with mere words.

As parents of young children, we directly instruct and dictate the results for disobedience and rewards for obedience. We give our young children instructions and we also provide the consequences for disobedience. Now, you want to begin becoming more of an older friend, or consultant, to your maturing son/daughter. So when you lead them into a time of reading the story of Exodus together, invite them to read it with you. Take turns reading verses out loud to each other. Take turns letting them lead the discussion in some of your times together. Give them a chance to prepare in advance some observances of how the Exodus story resembles a person's transition from childhood to adulthood. See if they can draw any comparisons to their own life. Make it an adventure or treasure hunt that the two of you (or three of you) pursue together.

A consultant helps someone see the logic or reasons for certain actions. A consultant points to the end results of certain choices. A consultant provides insight and perspective. However, a consultant does not have the authority to choose the course. A consultant seeks to inform and advise, but the client chooses. May God help you to become a trusted consultant to your new "client!"

One day, your child will be fully grown and out of your home. At that point he or she will be making all of his or her own choices. But won't it be wonderfully comforting for you to know that when that day comes your son/daughter has already demonstrated his/her own wisdom and preparedness for independence during these transition years? Here are some other ways to develop familiarity and love for God's word together:

1. Hopefully you and your student are already fairly familiar with Proverbs. Pull some examples from Proverbs that show consequences and results: "hand of the diligent shall rule" "the foolish despise correction," etc.
2. Read Psalm 1. What is God's law? Read some of God's laws (like those found in Exodus 20-26). Several good examples of rewards and consequences are found here.
3. Read Psalm 119 together. Discuss the consequences (end results) for choices mentioned in various verses.

The single most powerful person who can influence and encourage the early development of decision making skills in your son/daughter is you. Rise to the challenge and "engage the blade!"[8]

---

8 Frank Midgley's riding lawnmower term from chapter one.

Chapter 5 – The Blessing Rite of Passage – (Seventh grade – Ninth grade, Ages 12-15)

As I discussed earlier, the Hebrew culture recognizes a young man at age thirteen with a Bar mitzvah ("son of the commandments") ceremony and party, and a young woman with a Bat mitzvah ("daughter of the commandments") at age twelve. "The Blessing" is a Christian version of this rite of passage celebration.

God has designed your son/daughter biologically, emotionally, and spiritually to become a young adult at the outset of puberty. "The Blessing" reinforces what God has begun in your young adult's life. This section equips you with specific ways to mark, honor and affirm your son's or daughter's entry into adulthood.

I am thoroughly convinced that this can powerfully help you to instill within your young adult a clear awareness of identity and confidence at the very beginning of this typically tumultuous season. "The Blessing" will lay a solid foundation of trust and mutual respect for open communication between you and your young adult throughout the teenage years.

After spending six to twenty-four months in special conversations and times of reading together, using the recommendations from the "Preparing for Rite of Passage" section (Chapter 4), you and your son or daughter have most likely begun to feel a sense of anticipation, expectation and even readiness to recognize the end of childhood and the beginning of adulthood for him or her. Hopefully, this anticipation begins to awaken a drive within your son/daughter to want to take action in planning his/her own blessing ceremony.

As you begin planning for your big event, please remember it is most important to allow your son or daughter to have as much control and say so over the timing, place, and details as possible. They are the honoree, and this event should reflect their preferences and tastes.

Here are some helpful suggestions:

1. Preparations: Spend a minimum of six months preparing (see Chapter 4).
2. Planning the event: As a wedding is planned by the bride and groom, you want this Blessing ceremony to be largely planned by your son/daughter with some guidance from you. Let him/her choose the guest list, the menu, the venue, the music/entertainment, etc. This event should have his or her fingerprints all over it. If he/she is at a loss for any preferences, wait a few weeks, or even months, and help him or her become interested in planning this event. This blessing ceremony should be at a time when your child is already showing signs of maturity and seems truly ready to be recognized as a young adult. Ask permission to add people to the list that you want to invite, whom your budding adult does not originally think of. As much as possible, allow them to take leadership for this event using their own desires and interests. Communicate with them as a partner in making these plans.
3. Who: Everyone and every family is different. You may want to plan the event in two halves: a private meal and blessing time with close friends and family members,

preceding a formal ceremony and reception with a broader group of friends and acquaintances. Or you may want to hold the entire blessing event in your home with only close family and friends. Influential persons in a child's life should be invited, like favorite teachers from school or Sunday school, coaches, scout leaders, best friends' parents, close relatives, etc. Who you invite may also depend on the culture of your church, school, or community. Some churches celebrate with one large event, banquet style, for blessing several young men and women in one long evening. This can be very powerful. However, care should be taken to give each family their own special moment (fifteen to twenty minutes) to truly recognize and bless their own son/daughter.

4. Parent and Guest Participation: Parents and guests should prepare specific blessings. A blessing can be a specific Scripture verse or passage, a song sung or played, words spoken, prayers prayed, etc. Written blessings to be read in the event can also be helpful keepsakes for after the event is over. You might provide 3" x 5" cards to all guests as they arrive, so that everyone has an opportunity to write personal blessings and then leave them with the honoree. A powerful moment in the event can be when the young honoree sits in a chair in front of everyone present and each guest takes their turn, speaking words of affirmation and blessing.

5. The honoree should prepare a speech. This speech can include Scripture memorization, specific thanks, and statement of intentions, or goals for his/her life.

6. Each parent should give a speech of recognition, honor, affirmation and encouragement to their honoree, speaking directly to them in front of everyone.

7. Vows should be taken -- a vow by parents to "walk beside" their young adult child, and a vow by the honoree to partner with the parents in relationship decisions with the opposite gender, to include parents in dating choices and choice of a life partner. The audience should also rise to

their feet and vow to recognize the honoree as a young adult now and embrace the honoree into their adult world when possible. Remember, this event is intended to create a paradigm shift for the honoree, the parents, and the community surrounding the honoree. It is intended to change something on the inside of each person, so that in every way, the honoree is embraced and welcomed as the newest young adult in the community. *(See Appendix A for sample vows.)*

8. Gift – Parents should give a very special gift, something that will be valuable for a lifetime and held as an irreplaceable keepsake by the honoree.

9. When possible, live music should be included. Perhaps with a specifically selected song of dedication for the honoree, chosen by the parents; and/or a song of proclamation chosen by the honoree.

10. When guests are invited who may be unfamiliar with this type of event, an effort should be made to explain the event and its purpose both during the event itself (at the beginning) and in advance of the event (included with the invitation). The more that all guests can "buy in" to what is happening the more meaningful the event will be for the honoree and for everyone in attendance.

11. The party or reception afterwards should match the dignity of the event and the jubilance of welcoming a new adult into the community.

12. This is one of those occasions where the more money that can be spent on it, the better. The budget for this event should match the intentions for blessing the honoree. Extravagance is highly recommended.[9] Your young adult son/daughter is worth it.

---

[9] Just as we should budget and save for family vacations, for Christmas and birthday presents, and other predictable future expenses, so should you begin early on to budget and save for your son or daughter's rite of passage blessing ceremony.

13. Gifts and keepsakes are also recommended to be provided to everyone who attends. The honoree may want to give his/her closest friends each a special gift to memorialize this moment.

My Blessing Ceremony Experience - Heather McFarlin, 18

My Blessing ceremony was an experience like no other. It was like a fun, "sweet sixteen" party mixed with a ceremony that made me feel like I was ready to conquer the world!

I was excited for months before the ceremony -- buying a new dress, inviting all my friends, and just having a night focused completely on me! My birthday is in January, and this party was planned for October, which meant I was getting two parties just for me in one year!

Being twelve years old, a middle schooler in public school, it was difficult explaining this party to my friends. But once I told them that there would be live music, delicious food, and a limo picking us up afterwards, I had plenty of people wanting to come. It was also a reason to get all dressed up, and who doesn't love that?!

My mom took me shopping for my party attire, and I got a gorgeous pink, silky ball gown. Once I had the dress, I could barely contain my excitement for this big day. Like most twelve year old girls, I was extremely insecure about my appearance. But, when I put on that perfect dress, and pinned in the tiara my mom bought me, I felt like the most beautiful princess in the world.

At the ceremony, a friend of ours, Marty Goetz, played piano and sang some songs from his album. Marty was raised Jewish, now believes in Jesus, and he had a Bar mitzvah when he was thirteen. It was easy to relate to Marty and his songs, because he understood being a Christian and having this type of ceremony as well!

The night began with a gathering of our close church friends who really understood the meaning of the ceremony. They prayed for me and spoke blessings over my life.   Then Marty began playing as other guests entered the room.   The other guests consisted of school friends, neighbors, friends from dance class, extended family, and many others from our church and my parent's friends.

I felt a little awkward at first, because most of my friends did not really understand why they were there.   But, as the ceremony began, my dad explained the reasoning behind it, and everyone relaxed into accepting this new tradition.

Both of my parents spoke blessings over me in front of everyone. Marty sang. I spoke about my ambitions, dreams, and how my relationship with God and my parents was of utmost importance to me.   My dad and I made a commitment to keep each other in the loop as our lives progressed. He wanted to be the kind of dad who knew what guys were trying to date me. And I wanted to be the daughter who was comfortable with telling him about my daily life. This commitment built a level of trust that I still depend on as an eighteen year old college student.

Toward the end of the ceremony, all the women formed a tunnel with their arms, and my mom stood with me on one end while my dad stood at the other end. Since my mom has more of the caring and comforting role in my life, she stood on the side that symbolized my childhood.   As I walked through everyone celebrated my coming into adulthood, my dad welcomed me on the other end.

After the ceremony was over, everyone indulged in delicious treats. Some people gave me gifts, but for the most part everyone just enjoyed each others' company.

A limousine picked up about ten of my friends and me and drove us around town for an hour. We rode around Murfreesboro screaming with excitement and thoroughly enjoying *every* second of the ride.

One year before my blessing ceremony, the church we were attending in Franklin, Abounding Grace Center, held a large blessing ceremony for many of my older friends.   I went to the ceremony, and it made me look forward to when I would be old enough to have one.   Because I had witnessed the church's blessing ceremony, I was prepared to have one of my own when the time came. My dad and I also spent time during the year before my ceremony reading through Proverbs and going on outings together. We would get coffee and have "daddy-daughter talks" about life.

The level of trust that was built between my parents and me at my blessing ceremony has really made our relationship closer. I felt that they recognized me as an adult, and they began relating to me in that way as well.

If I could change anything about my blessing ceremony, it would be the level of understanding my friends and extended family had about it. It would have been much easier if they knew all about the ceremony and were comfortable with the idea. Now , however, they are aware of what a blessing ceremony truly is. So, should it ever come up in their lives again, they will be more prepared. Altogether, my blessing ceremony was a wonderful experience, and I hope to share what I have gotten from it with my own children someday.

Dad's Commentary on Heather's Blessing Ceremony

About six months before Heather's blessing ceremony, she told Linette and me that she wanted a limousine ride after her ceremony. We encouraged her to call some companies in the yellow pages and find out how much it cost. She learned that it would cost $80 to rent for one hour. We told her that we would not pay for this, but she was welcome to earn the money and save for it to treat herself in this way.

She babysat, taught beginner ballet lessons, washed cars, and picked up other odd jobs to earn the money. About three weeks before her ceremony, she had saved enough money. But then she told us one day, "I have decided I don't want to spend all that money on a one hour ride." She had learned the value of a dollar!

Through a remarkable set of circumstances, we personally met a limousine company owner just a week before her big event. When Heather told the owner about her upcoming blessing ceremony and her desire to ride in a limousine, the limousine owner replied, "Honey, I believe your first limousine ride is going to be on the house!" This dream came true in answer to prayer and as a wonderful example of God demonstrating His kindness in Heather's life! A limousine ride may seem trivial or superfluous. But, God is real, and He truly cares for us personally and the personal details of our lives.

My Blessing Ceremony Experience - Mary Anna McFarlin, 14

I was recognized as an adult through a blessing ceremony called a Bat-Barakah (Hebrew for "daughter of the blessing"), and it was definitely a blessing. It was held in a large pavilion on October 25, 2009.

My father opened up the evening by welcoming everyone. He talked a little about what this ceremony meant and told everyone why they were there. Then he asked my mother and me to stand up next to him. As I stood there in my light pink ball gown, the same one my sister wore at her blessing ceremony, my parents poured blessings over me.

After the blessings my dad's friend, Anthony Skinner, sang and played on his guitar the song "Anyway" by Martina McBride. It was beautiful. Next, I made a promise to my parents that I would let them be involved in my life. I pray that I will continue to keep this commitment as I go into high school.

Then, I gave a speech that I had prepared. In it I thanked my friends, teachers, and family for being there for me when I needed them. I also read one of my favorite verses -- "Be quick to listen, slow to speak, and slow to become angry" (James 1:19). I talked a little about how I would apply this in my life. I remember feeling so nervous about speaking to all those people, but as I continued to talk, I felt better.

The next thing we had planned was really cool. My mother asked all the women and girls to come up to the front and make two rows facing each other. Then she asked them to put their hands up to make an arch. I stood on the end with the little girls and my mom stood at the end with the adult women. I walked through the tunnel resembling my passing from childhood to adulthood. Everyone cheered when I came out of the tunnel. I felt fantastic.

A little later my dad handed out note cards to everyone. They all sat down and wrote nice things about me on them. Like, "Thanks for being my friend," or "I am so glad that you are in my life." Everything they said really made me feel good.

This ceremony isn't just a party. It takes preparation. The main two things that prepared me for it were going to my sister's blessing ceremony and spending time with my dad. He would take me out somewhere, just the two of us, and he would talk to me about things of this world and life. Yes, sometimes it was awkward, but in the end our relationship was growing, and I could feel that. Now, since the ceremony has been over I feel more comfortable communicating with my parents. I know that my story sounds like everything went just perfectly, and it was all peaches and cream, but that's not true. If I could do it over again I would send out the invitations earlier so that more people could come. Also, I would have had more white lights strung up to make a beautiful design in the pavilion ceiling.

This ceremony left me feeling strong and confident.

Dad's Commentary on Mary Anna's Blessing Ceremony

An impetus for me writing this book is the low response we received to invitations for Mary Anna's Blessing Ceremony. I truly hope churches and schools will use this book to encourage all parents to adopt this type of tradition for their teenagers. Our oldest daughter grew up in such a church. Nearly all of her friends had blessing ceremonies. Since we had moved to a different city, Mary Anna was the only one among her friends who was honored in this way. The cumulative impact of a community of faith honoring their teenagers with rites of passages is wonderful and powerful.

Also, Mary Anna had asked me if I would slow dance with her

when Anthony played the song "Anyway" during the ceremony. I had told her before that I might feel too uncomfortable, but I would wait and see. Unfortunately, I did feel too self-conscious about it. So, I did not get up and dance with Mary Anna in front of everyone. When all was done, and we returned home, Mary Anna walked straight to our i-Mac in the den (where our music is stored). She turned on the song, "Anyway," by Martina McBride, and said "Come here, Daddy." She asked me to dance with her. We danced in the living room, with just our family present (my wife and her siblings) all the way through. Mary Anna looked me in the eye and said, "Thank you Daddy." Oh man! It tore me up. I regret that I didn't have the courage to give her what she wanted when everyone else was present. My friend Anthony later told me, "you robbed us all of that." He was so right.

A Final Word on the Ceremony Itself -- You Have the Right to Choose the Scale of Your Blessing Ceremony!

Hopefully you now are familiar with the traditional Bar/Bat mitzvah as it is celebrated by Jewish families. Typically, this is an extravagant affair and a very big deal! There are many ways to bless your teenager, however, and honor his/her passing from childhood to adulthood. Each teen has a unique personality. Each family has unique circumstances. Different seasons of life have varying degrees of open time in the schedule and amounts of disposable income, with varying schedules and varying budgets. I encourage you to realize that you can bless your child with ANY scale of celebration. Don't make the mistake of dismissing the idea due to stress or busyness or lack of funds.

One of my closest friends told me of a Christmas he experienced as a child. That year, his parents wrote him a personal letter. Likewise, his two brothers and his sister received their own personal letter. When he came to the Christmas tree that Christmas morning, he found his letter in a sealed envelope. The letter listed all the things his parents wanted to buy for him, and explained that they did not have the money to make these purchases. The letter went on to tell my friend how special he was, and how much his parents loved him. My friend remembers sitting with all of his siblings in silence and each one reading their own letters in silence together with their parents in the room. He remembers this Christmas as his favorite and most special Christmas ever!

Another of my close friends told me that when his son turned thirteen, he wrote a letter to him. He invited his wife, and all of his children to gather around the dinner table. Nothing else was happening except the reading of this letter. He read this letter out loud to his thirteen year old son in the presence of the family. This was his coming of age rite of passage celebration for his son. The mother confirmed that this thirteen year old young man was beaming with joy and affirmation during and after the reading of this letter.

In this chapter, I described a typical blessing ceremony and celebration in the tradition of a Jewish Bar/Bat mitzvah. Having said that, I encourage you to observe the main point: Honor your teenager with extravagant words. Acknowledge his/her passage into adulthood. Extend yourself emotionally. Recognize him/her in front of others in a manner that builds him/her up. This can happen on any scale!

Also, if you are an empty nester, all of your children are "grown and gone." However, it is never too late to recognize their adulthood and bless the uniqueness of your adult child with a solemn moment and celebration. Adapt your blessing to your family and your stage in life. Let your heart hear the spirit of the message of this book and know that it is never too late, at least until you die!

Chapter 6 – Sexual Purity (Eighth grade – Ages 13-14)

Let's talk about sex. It is a physical act. Sex is an emotional act. It is equally a spiritual act. Sex also is a comprehensive/successive act.

1. Reproduction – Sex makes babies! Yes, it is important for you to tell this fact to your son/daughter. Most likely this will come as no surprise. And hopefully you have already talked a little about this (earlier than the summer before eighth grade begins). Ideally, your child will hear and learn about the reproductive nature of sex from you first and foremost, rather than from peers or media or school. So tell them. Tell them about the egg and the ovaries and the cycle a woman has monthly. Tell them about the sperm, the race, the conception and the forty weeks of development within the womb. And yes, tell them how God created us to fit together and make all of this happen.

2. Appeal – Sex has appeal! Please discuss the appeal of sex with your son and/or daughter. Discuss the affection, the affirmation, the emotional bond that happens when a man

and woman have sex. Discuss the vulnerability and intimacy. Help him/her understand the value and importance of this experience being shared only with one faithful, loving, life-partner. Acknowledge to them the powerful nature of the sex drive.

3. Differences between Men and Women – I have heard it said, "Women need a reason, men need a place." Hopefully this is an exaggeration of our differences! However, it seems to be true that men are stimulated by sight, while women are stimulated by touch and a feeling of security and being cared for. I like this illustration: a man's sexuality is like a box with one switch for "on" or "off." A woman's sexuality is like an airplane pilot's dashboard with dozens and dozens of buttons. A woman may crave touch and attention for the sole purpose of wanting affection and comfort. A man often interprets affection as a sexually arousing invitation. He can quickly move beyond where a woman was prepared to go, misinterpreting her affection as sexual arousal. Knowing these differences will dramatically improve your son's/daughter's awareness of themselves, and the message they send to people around them by what they wear, how they act, etc. For example, if a young woman wants to be treated respectfully as a person, rather than as a sex object, then it is recommended that she fully clothe herself, and not go to school wearing short shorts and a small little halter top, or mini-mini-skirt with a very low cut, unbuttoned blouse. Talk about these differences between the way men are wired sexually and the way women are wired sexually. How can these differences lead to misunderstandings? How can knowing these differences help determine the way you act around opposite gender friends? Ask your son/daughter, "Have you noticed some of these differences at work already in your school or church group?"

4. Sex is an act that includes flirting, talking intimately, touching, kissing, caressing, fondling, stripping, and ultimately intercourse. All of these are part of the act of

"having sex." Sex is a succession of these activities, each one leading toward the next. Your son or daughter needs to know this. When a young man and young woman have a commitment to "not have sex until marriage," but then they lay horizontal together and kiss and caress, it is like sitting in a powerful car with one foot on the brakes and one foot pushing the gas pedal to the floor. The fact is they are having the beginning phase of sex. And their hearts are bonding. Sex is meant to knit our souls together, and it does. The farther down the "sex road" they travel, the closer they are to arriving at that destination. Therefore, it is important for you to explain to your son or daughter this reality, to help them choose wisely.

Now here are some recommended conversations and activities to help illustrate these points and help your son or daughter see the end result of sexual activity.

Paste a pink heart and a blue heart together (construction paper and glue). Allow for time to dry.

1. Tell a story of "Johnny" and "Gina" choosing to hold hands, kiss, and become sexually active. Describe how this causes their hearts to be "knit together," because sexuality involves the emotions and our souls equally as much as it involves our bodies. Eventually Johnny and Gina begin to argue and fight until they ultimately break up. Ask you son/daughter to try to pull the pink heart off of the blue heart, while you hold the blue heart. Most likely you will each end up with a torn heart that has pieces of the other still attached. This illustrates how sexual activity ending in breakup leaves a piece of each person's heart attached to the other – a consequence of not abstaining until marriage.
2. Do a google search on Herpes II, Human Papilloma Virus (genital warts) and sexually transmitted diseases. Herpes II affects 28% of all Americans (more than one in four). It is spread by skin to skin contact and highly contagious. Human Papilloma Virus, or HPV, is the fastest spreading and most

contagious STD, also caused by skin to skin contact. It is the cause of 99% of cervical cancer in women.[10] After sharing some of these facts, ask your child the question, "Does sex cause disease?" The correct answer is NO. *Only sex outside of marriage causes disease.* The act of sex between a faithfully married man and faithfully married woman does not spread disease. Faithfully married couples do not get sexually transmitted diseases, no matter how often they have sex together. Sex is good, and it is God's gift to us. It was never intended to spread disease. It is the *misuse* of sex which leads to bad consequences.

3. Take your driver's license out of your pocket. Ask your child, "What does this allow me to do?" "Can I drive anytime?" (i.e. night, day, midnight, 4 a.m., etc.) "Can I drive in any state?"(Tennessee, Texas, Hawaii, etc.) "Can I drive any truck, SUV, van, car, sports car?" – So far the answer to all of these questions is "Yes." Now ask, "Can I drive as fast as I want to as often as I want to?" -- correct answer: "No." Because if I do, this license can be revoked, and I can lose my privilege. So, with adulthood comes freedom. But freedom always has limits and responsibilities. As long as I honor those rules (God's commands), I continue to enjoy great freedom. This is also true of sex.

Breaking God's commands is not like civil disobediences (i.e. driving over the speed limit). I can sometimes drive over the speed limit and not get caught, not suffer any negative consequences. However, breaking God's commands (sinning) always results in negative consequences.

A mother should talk in detail with a daughter, and a father should talk in detail with a son, about this topic. However, it is equally important for each parent to discuss these things with each child. The father needs to speak about this topic with his daughter, and a mother needs to speak about this topic with her son. Having a healthy conversation with the opposite gender

---

[10] Again, thanks to Dr. Omar Hamada for these medical facts.

parent helps remove shame from this topic.   The father is affirming his daughter's gender identity by talking with her about her sexuality in an appropriate and candid manner. The mother is revealing the discreetness and sweetness of this topic to her son by talking with him about this topic in an appropriate and candid manner.

For more information and resources to help you talk with your teenager about sex, check out *www.silverringthing.com*.   Under "About SRT" and "Info for Parents" you will find the "NEXT Parent Study Guide".   This is a valuable discussion tool that costs less than six dollars.   Also at *www.abstinence.net,* under "store" and "brochures" you will find several valuable discussion guides for thirty cents each!

Chapter 7 - The Driving Contract (Ninth Grade – Ages 14-15)

If you do not have a habit of using profanity, good for you. If you have successfully overcome the habit, teaching your fifteen year old how to drive can cause you to relapse! Driving is just one of those high risk activities that we tend to take for granted because we drive every day, over and over again. Driving is dangerous. Driving without experience can be deadly. However, this can be another marvelous rite of passage experience for you to have with your teenager.

Preparing your teen to drive can literally be a life-saving exercise. Moving vehicle accidents are the number one cause of teenage deaths in America -- 40% of teenage deaths in America are the result of MVA's. I personally had very little training when I was fifteen and sixteen, though I did have a lot of experience. My parents often let me drive, but I was very argumentative. I am certain that I contested their every comment. By the time I was married at the age of twenty-two, I had totaled three cars, and had seven traffic accidents. It reminds me of a good basketball coach who asked the team, "Does practice make perfect?" We all answered, "Yes!" "No, practice does not make perfect, but the right kind of practice does!" he retorted.

I have heard parents say, "Well, you know they are going to have an accident, every new driver does!" Nonsense! Training your teen to drive properly involves more than just scooting over and letting them take the wheel. If you will "engage the blade" and take the time to truly train them, you can dramatically lower their risk of an accident. This can also be a wonderful bonding experience. Driver's training creates the perfect opportunity to establish yourself as a respected and valuable consultant in their life -- perhaps a life-saving consultant!

Here are some suggestions.

Require your trainee to read a driving guide. Every state publishes their own "rules of the road" and provides guides for new drivers. Your car insurance company has these as well. Ask your agent. Go online. Some guides are for sale, but either from your state, your insurance company, or a Google search online, you will find plenty of free beginner driving guides to choose from. Explain to your "trainee" that they must read this first and answer some questions on it before you put them behind the wheel. Most of these guides have sample tests with them.

Establish right up front that during this training, and until you say otherwise, you are the boss. You are the instructor now. Homeschool parents and/or owners of businesses understand the requirement for mandating that children learn to relate to you in a different role at times than just "parent/child." I think it helps to actually wear a hat. You are getting ready to discuss something very significant with them, which can have heavy consequences if ignored -- traffic rules! You want to make sure they are listening with "new ears" and not just rolling their eyes and saying, "Oh Dad/Mom, whatever."

When my oldest daughter was six we home-schooled her. On Tuesday's she attended a full day of class with other home schooled children. Her teacher always commented on how well behaved she was -- she diligently completed her assignments and followed instructions without any resistance. Wow! My wife was surprised, because her experience during the other four days a week seemed like constant struggle. One night she was describing to me the battles of the day, and I suggested that she put on a hat the next morning when it was school time – Her teacher's hat!

When class began the next day, Linette put on her hat and explained, "When Mommy has this hat on, I am no longer Mommy, I am now Teacher." She went on to explain that the same rules that applied to Tuesday School, applied when Mommy had on the hat. She explained, "If you disobey, then you get a strike. Three strikes and you are out, which means you go to the principal's office."

In our case at home, I was the principal. I gave spankings. Our six year old listened carefully. At the end of Linette's explanation, she rose up out of her seat, walked around the table, took the hat off of Linette's head and threw it down the hallway, saying "that's a stupid hat!" To which Linette replied, "Strike one!"

Find a way to welcome your driving-trainee into a new role with you as instructor and he or she as student when you are teaching them how to drive. You are changing roles and asking them to change roles with you. Set aside this time as deliberate and special time for driving instruction. It will help your son/daughter to embrace what you have to offer, and it will empower them to have confidence when they begin to learn how to drive.

Find a secluded, low-risk place. Use a remote location, like a large industrial parking lot on a Sunday afternoon, or a wide-open straight country road with no other cars for miles, or a well-lit mall parking lot when the mall is closed. Allow your student to get comfortable just controlling the car, and relax. Set them up so that they can make mistakes with no consequence and cause you no worries. Put them into a stress-free location and setting, so that you can be calm, cool and collected! Enjoy it. Laugh.

Help your teenager get comfortable with themselves behind the wheel and the feel of the car. After some practice, I personally like smaller, country or curvy roads because when they encounter on-coming traffic, everyone is driving slowly (i.e. 30 miles or less). I actually taught one of my daughters to drive when we were on vacation for a week in a place with very curvy roads. Because the road was so curvy, no one was driving fast, everyone was driving very slowly and this made it less stressful for her and me. She gained tremendous confidence that week!

Practice often. Competence breeds confidence. Driving well comes primarily from lots of experience. The more experience the better. Encourage every opportunity for your teenager to be behind the wheel in all types of weather and road conditions. By the time he or she has his or her license, you want them to be very experienced!

Tell your son or daughter that you are proud of them. Tell them you are confident that they can do this. Tell them they have what it takes and that their time has arrived. Assure them that they can do this and that you have confidence in their preparedness to learn how to drive.

Once they have gained some confidence, take a trip to a large city. Tell them to never, ever pull over on the side of an interstate unless they absolutely have no other choice. Always exit off of the interstate first. Too much can and does happen when cars are traveling over sixty miles an hour. People from smaller towns or remote states who have not travelled in big cities do not realize how much peril they are in when they pull over on a busy downtown interstate. Train your teen to avoid danger. Build their confidence by guiding them through busy six lane traffic situations. You want them fully prepared and experienced with every possible traffic situation.

When you are confident that your son/daughter is competent to drive, then help them contact your car insurance company and learn how much it will cost to add them as a driver. Encourage them to ask the insurance company if a driving contract matters in the price, or if grade point average, or driver's ed class, changes the price. Ask them for a full reporting of the costs and options for reducing these costs. This is all part of helping them to decide for themselves that they need to enroll in a driver's ed class. Help them come to this conclusion themselves. You are teaching decision making skills.

Draw up a driving contract with them. Agree on all of the terms and conditions together, and have them sign it. Sign it yourself. Make a copy for them to keep, and you keep the original. Agree to review this contract once or twice a year, as you see fit. I recommend *www.parentingteendrivers.com* for the most comprehensive resource I have found on preparing your teen to be a safe driver. *(See Appendix B in this book for a sample driving contract.)*

Now, help them obtain a driver's license. Try to arrange a separate ride home for yourself when the test and driving exam is over. Hopefully, by the time you help them obtain their license, you will have the confidence in your trained driver to simply throw them the keys to drive away all alone as soon as they have a license. You want them THAT prepared BEFORE they have a license. This is truly a life saving exercise! They will never forget that moment of freedom, and the confidence you placed in them! You are giving your son/daughter every probability for successful, safe driving, and now they have their reward. And you have yours – a prepared, trained, and experienced teenage driver.

Chapter 8: Work – Delivering Value to the Marketplace (Tenth Grade, Age 16)

One summer day, when I was sixteen, I remember being on the court at a tennis team practice. I just happened to be playing on the end closest to the clubhouse, when my friend Lisa Eischeid ran out to the courts shouting, "The movie theatre needs to hire someone. Does anyone want a job?" About six of us shouted, "I do!" Lisa responded, "Hunter McFarlin was first. You got the job, be there at 7:00 tonight sharp, and don't wear jeans!"

I started out selling popcorn, cokes, and candy, and eventually learned how to do every job there, including changing the giant sign high above the street and splicing the film together when new movies arrived on Thursday nights. Only recently, after the death of the man who managed that theatre for over forty years, have I had to pay for movie tickets. These were great experiences and provided me with life lessons, cash and perks.

Raising a teenager and never allowing them to feel the need for generating cash flow can prove crippling. Teenagers absolutely need money for many reasons -- ballgames, driving (gas, oil change, maintenance, insurance, the cost of the car itself), dances, prom, dates, movies, eating out, Starbucks, clothes, shoes, sunglasses, school functions, school rings, school annuals, graduations, concerts, clubs, trips, gifts for birthday parties, school lunches, pizza, and gifts for Bar/Bat mitzvahs! This very long list of financial "necessities" is hopefully the very thing that motivates your son/daughter to want to become productive -- now! Teenagers can be very resourceful and perfectly capable of working and generating cash flow in many creative ways.

So, foster creativity. Encourage your teenager to appreciate that much of what they want costs money, and challenge them to find ways to earn it. Their felt need for cash is God's gift to them. Don't interfere with it. Proverbs 16:26 says, "The hunger of a man drives him to work." All that most teenagers need is some encouragement and belief in themselves. When they bring up something they want that costs money, let your first words to them be: "Yes, you should absolutely have that! And you have exactly what it takes to earn the money (generate the cash flow) to buy it."

Teach them to believe that with hard work, diligence, and faith anything is possible. "I want you to have those things (or do those things) and I am here to help you find ways for you to make it happen." They can get a job, cut grass, deliver dry cleaning for attorneys and other "white collars," provide a recycling pick-up route, design a website, edit a video, set up chairs before weekly meetings, wait tables, deliver pizza, pump gas, etc. There are all kinds of ways for a young, energetic, talented teenager to be productive – outside the home! Chores at home and earning allowance is good. But hopefully your teenager is eager to begin to drive, around the age of sixteen, and it is time for them to get out there and find a place in the world where they can make a difference -- for profit!

Economics and working in the marketplace provide us with accountability, opportunity and the perfect environment for discovering and fulfilling our calling. If you are the type of parent who has the means and the tendency to protect your son/ daughter from lack, then maybe it's time for you to withhold some funds and help your teenager "cowboy/cowgirl up!"

If you are the type of parent who lives under financial pressure, you may have a tendency to always say, "we can't afford that." May God give you hope that you can share with your son or daughter. My mother used to always say, "where there is a will, there is a way!" Pray to God for help and inspiration for the provision of what your son/daughter wants. Teach them to believe in God, who can make a way. He is creative and able to help you and your sixteen year old experience the fulfillment of their heart's desire.

One summer, while I was in college, I wanted a motorcycle. My mother and my fiancée were against me having one. Plus I had no money to buy one. A local teenage- night club was raffling one to raise money. I bought two tickets for four dollars. As I filled them out, I thought, "Lord, you know the desire of my heart." I won! It was a Nighthawk 450. Two years later, I wanted to go to Europe on a mission trip behind the Iron Curtain. I also wanted to study the German language, in Germany. I had read *God's Smuggler,* by Brother Andrew, and some books by Loren Cunningham, founder of *Youth With A Mission.* These books filled me with faith that God could do financial miracles and make a way for me to fulfill my dream.

I put my car up for sale, I put my motorcycle up for sale, I prayed, and I worked. I felt impressed by God not to let anyone know that I needed money. When people asked me how much money I needed for the trip, I always told them what I had for sale and that I was trusting God to provide. It was amazing to see where the money came from. I literally sold both the motorcycle and the car only one week before I left town, enabling me to pay off a loan I used to buy the airplane tickets and register for these trips. I left the country with $1,000 more than I needed. It was truly a very rich summer indeed!

Earning is important. Saving is important. Tithing is important. Giving is important. Budgeting is important. Investing is important. Sometimes borrowing may be important. As a financial planner I have seen people over do it in every category. I have also seen people suffer as a result of not understanding each of these uses of money. Help your teenager get a job or start a business. Be creative. Encourage their creativity. Or, be boring. Any job is a good job for a season. Encourage them to give, and to tithe. Teach them how to budget. Teach them to save. Teach them to invest. Help them understand borrowing.

My favorite authors on making and using money wisely are Craig Hill, Rabbi Daniel Lapin, Ron Blue, Larry Burkette, Dave Ramsey, and Robert Kiyosaki. Kiyosaki has a book titled *Rich Dad, Poor Dad for Teenagers*. Craig Hill has a book called *Wealth, Riches, and Money, Biblical Principals of Finance*. Rabbi Daniel Lapin has a book entitled *Thou Shall Prosper*, and Dave Ramsey offers a Bible study for young people on what God has to say about money, *Generation Change (www.daveramsey.com)*. I encourage you to read these and share them with your son/daughter.

One of the best learning tools I have experienced is the "Cash Flow Game" from *www.richdad.com* and the "Cash Flow for Kids Game" (ages six to twelve) by Robert Kiyosaki. My family has played these games for years. They impart wisdom and understanding about money. "In all your getting, get understanding!" (Proverbs 4:7)

I have been poor and I have had more than enough. I wish that I could say, like Paul, that I have learned to be content in all things. I haven't. But I have learned that God is a God of abundance. There is always enough. Sometimes we just need to press into Him and hang in there believing for His provision, being thankful for what we have.

Help your teenager to get out into the world where they can make a difference. And help them learn to get paid to do it. They must begin to master their own money! A job also teaches them about getting along with people, following directions, and dealing with difficult managers and inner-office/job politics. These are all valuable lessons for them to begin learning now, rather than later.

This sixteenth year is also another excellent opportunity to celebrate your son/daughter with a sweet sixteen birthday party. Many families do this. Often the event includes a four-wheel gift! I highly recommend this. At the time of my oldest daughter's sweet sixteen, we were not able to buy her a car, nor was she able to pay for one.

We did, however, have a very nice sweet sixteen party complete with live band, sharply dressed young men and beautifully dressed young women. She planned this event. She was honored by it. Seven months later we were able to deliver the car we wanted her to have, just in time for her junior year of high school to begin. At the party I briefly spoke some words of blessing to my daughter, in front of all her friends, and read a brief passage of Scripture. She later told Linette and me how much she appreciated all that we did to make her sixteenth birthday special.

You know the phrase - *carpe diem*. With teenagers, seize every opportunity you can to celebrate and honor them. Be extravagant. Spend as much money as possible. Speak abundant words of blessing, words of praise, words of affirmation over them. Think of the Father's heart toward you -- His generosity and His extravagance. Express this same generosity and extravagance to your son/daughter for their sweet sixteenth!

Linette and I took extra measures to be able to buy our daughter a brand new car. Some of our friends warned us that she would only wreck it. Others scolded us for being so "wasteful." I told her that this is her first car, and she deserves this and even more. I told my daughter that I hoped she wouldn't have a wreck, but that it would change nothing in how I felt about or thought of her if she were to have one. I told her that sometimes bad things happen to everyone, and if she were to have a wreck, not to worry. So far, she is driving wreck-free!

May God continue to show her His kindness. My wife and I always have great comfort in her safety and the car's reliability. Our confidence is in God's faithfulness and in the newness of her car. She is blessed. We required her to work and earn money and save her own money to have a certain amount in her car fund. Until she did this, we would not buy her a car. Her friends told her she had the "meanest parents," because she was having to work so hard and was not able to spend any of her money.

Actually, she could have spent money if she wanted to, but she had decided that she wanted a car. We suggested the car to her that we wanted for her. Once we saw her approval, that it was more than she would have asked for herself, we allowed her to pick it out. When she did pick it out, we bought the next model up with extra features. I believe this sends a message to her heart that she is valuable and cherished. She is filled with dignity and honor for herself.

Chapter 9 - Family Heritage and Legacy – Age 17

Events of child abuse have their highest occurrence at the ages of three and seventeen. These are the primary years in which children or young men and women seek to establish themselves in their own identity. Uniqueness and individuality emerge with new force. Is the world ready for me? Are you as a parent ready to see your child as an adult? If not, sparks will fly! Because, ready or not, here he/she comes! Now more then ever a seventeen year old needs to be recognized and taken seriously as an adult member of the family. He/she is looking for validation as a unique individual adult. A seventeen year old wants to be relied upon and reckoned with.

Sometimes, due to painful family history, secrets are kept. Or sometimes, due to powerful and/or wealthy family circumstances, secrets are kept. Other times, just inconvenience, or awkward issues, lead to avoidance and cover up. Often we have very good reasons for withholding information from children. A seventeen year old, however, is no longer a child. Profound relief can come to a family when the "circle of trust" is extended to a prepared seventeen year old. Almost always the revealing of family heritage (good, bad and ugly) brings relief and explanation to a seventeen year old who has sensed these things for some time but not known why or exactly what these feelings have meant. Children instinctively blame themselves for any sense of wrongness. When you reveal family secrets to your seventeen year old, it often let's them off the hook. They learn from your disclosure that their feelings of inner conflict are not self-imposed. Your disclosure gives them an answer to ambiguous turmoil.

What if your child is adopted? This seventeenth year is an excellent time to tell the story. Is there an undisclosed step-parent in the house? This is a perfect year for the step-parent and spouse together to tell the story of the other (absent) biological parent. Did something violent or tragic happen to this child when he/she was younger (i.e. molestation, kidnapping, being lost for some time, major surgery, tragic accident, etc.)? This seventeenth year is the right time to tell what you know and seek professional help for delving into exactly what happened. Is there extreme family wealth, or fame that is not yet disclosed? The age of seventeen is an excellent time to help your son/daughter begin to cope with weighty issues.

Realities like these are already impacting every member of your family. By the time a teenager turns seventeen, they are often more aware of these family "secrets" than you think (the proverbial "elephant in the room"). You can help recognize them as a young adult by allowing them to begin bearing some of the weight of these family secrets openly, with your help. While they are living at home under your roof, you have the best opportunity to walk in this knowledge with them and guide them. This can be a powerful time of sharing adulthood with them. The rewards for both of you will far outweigh the inconvenience and emotional energy this will require of you as a parent.

Perhaps your family doesn't have any dramatic facts or circumstances. Use this age to share the family tree and discuss family stories, throughout the family's history. Your seventeen year old is hoisting his/her sails up to catch the wind, beginning to try themselves out in the world. When you give them knowledge of where they are from and who they are from, and what they carry with them in their family heritage, you give them roots and equip them with a point of reference.

So trust them! Empower them! Let them in on it. Never be afraid to seek professional help when needed. If you contributed to something painful in their past, then the most powerful thing you can do is bring it out into the light and tell them the truth. Tell them you are sorry. Admit the mistake you made. Tell them your regrets. Ask their forgiveness. And seek professional help. This can truly be a powerful breakthrough of freedom and life and healing for you, your seventeen year old, and your entire family. Don't let them grow older and leave the house without helping them now to face these things!

Many of us want to be defined by where we are headed (heaven!). However, knowing where we came from and who we came from helps clarify what material we have to work with. What are your family secrets? Jesus said, "You will know the truth, and the truth will set you free" (John 8:32). Sometimes facing the truth and revealing the truth takes courage. We hope this section empowers you to courageously introduce your young adult son or daughter to their own personal family heritage.

The sooner you do this the better, so that they can get on with their aspirations! You have the power to give your children roots and wings.

BONUS: *The Generational Sticking Power of a Culture of Blessing*

The Jewish culture is rich with traditions of blessing and celebration. God commands his people to celebrate seven holy days, or holidays, during the calendar year. Many of these are week long holidays. When Sarah weaned Isaac, Abraham threw a feast. The Bar/Bat mitzvah for Jewish young men and women is usually a solemn ceremony followed by an extravagant celebration! Have you ever been to a Jewish wedding? If so, then most likely you know the jubilation of men dancing. The weekly Friday evening Shabbat meal is another time in which Jewish fathers bless their children (see the bonus chapter at the end of this book). I love these people and their customs!

Imagine the self-esteem and confidence a child must have being raised in family traditions of Friday night blessings and several week long holidays throughout the year. Imagine the sense of identity, the inner-knowledge, of "who I am" and "who I belong to" that these traditions instill. I am asking you to peer in through a window at these traditions and ask, "what impact does this have on the human psyche?", and "Is there something here for me and my family?"

Throughout the history of the world no people group on earth has been persecuted, enslaved, hunted, or disenfranchised as much and as often as the Jewish people. In fact, from 70 A.D. to 1948, a one thousand eight hundred and seventy eight year span, the Jewish people had no geographical location to call home. They were disenfranchised for over eighteen centuries. Most nations in the earth were hostile to them during this long span of time. Yet, the Jewish culture prevailed. The identity of this people persisted and their traditions remain intact to this day. I believe this is partly because of their family culture of blessing![11]

---

[11] See an interesting timeline at the Israel Ministry of Foreign Affairs website: *http://www.mfa.gov.il* and select "History of Israel."

Chapter 10 - Manhood/Womanhood (Twelfth Grade)

For me, this eighteenth year with my oldest daughter was mixed with sadness and relief. Relief -- to see how mature and capable and wise she is. Sadness -- to realize that this is her last year in our home (maybe forever, but definitely for the next few years). Linette and I deliberately have no rules, no curfews, no restraints that we mandate for our eighteen year old. She is an adult now. As far as rules go, we treat her as a tenant. She comes and goes and does as she pleases.

Of course, she has earned this freedom. She studies diligently and earns mostly A's. She is conscientious in her leadership roles at school. She consistently attends church and her youth ministry small group. She helps with laundry, dishes, and housework, as well as with watching our younger children. She is reliable and trustworthy. We feed her, clothe her, house her, and provide her with money. We ask her to participate in our family and household responsibilities and that she communicate with us.

She does so willingly. She also faithfully calls us to tell us if she is headed out of town with friends for dinner or some event. She asks us if she can be away from dinner for a date or time with friends. She calls us when her plans change. She lets us know if she wants to spend the night with one of her friends, or if she wants them to spend the night in our home. She asks us each time she plans a date with her boyfriend. There is open communication between us. Rarely do we ask her to alter her plans. We try to always say "yes." We also let her know when we would like to have her around more, because she has a tendency to get very busy! We are confident that she lives with self-control.

We ask her to be at dinner with us on Friday nights, when we have a simple way of practicing the traditional Jewish Shabbat meal as a family. We ask her to have breakfast with us Saturday mornings and Sunday afternoon lunch. She often babysits for us when we have a date or are out of town for a night or weekend. She has one morning a week that she takes her younger siblings to school in the morning, and one afternoon a week that she picks them up. Occasionally, we ask her to run an errand for us. But we respect the fullness of her schedule. We treat her as an adult guest in our home. We trust her.

We know her friends. They are often over at our house. Heather asked us to allow her to have her eighteenth birthday party here, in our home. We were host to over forty eighteen year olds! It was a delightful night. They were terrific young people. We enjoyed hearing their fun from the other end of the house. The quality of her friends reveals a lot to us about her.

This eighteenth year should most closely resemble life for you and for your eighteen year old as it will when he or she is nineteen and out of the house. Hopefully, when they leaves home, their lifestyle will change very little. You want life for your son or daughter away from the home (next year) to be very similar to what it is now. This similarity shows you that they can handle life on their own; it shows them that they can handle it as well. Also, when dilemmas come up, you are in close proximity to deal with it.

The only real "test of the wills" I can think of that we have with Heather now is regarding plans for her future (i.e. which college to attend). The fact is she has good choices from good schools with good scholarship offers. Even in this conflict we have open and honest dialogue. Linette and I both feel heard by her and respected. We also respect her. We are confident that she walks with God, and He leads her.

The preparations recommended in this book for the sixth and seventh grades, the blessing ceremony recommended in the eighth grade, and the rest of the exercises, all lead up to helping you to produce a healthy, mature eighteen year old who knows his or her value and purpose. I believe it is important to have a final party celebrating your son or daughter. We chose to do this as a graduation party which included a very nice gift and a big trip!

The party was planned in conjunction with one of her best friends, Stephanie. Stephanie's parents wanted to celebrate as eagerly as we did. We had a cookout. We invited extended family members, neighbors and friends. She and Stephanie planned a water balloon/squirt gun fight. Everyone had lots of fun. My wife's parents had planned a nice trip for their fiftieth wedding anniversary. They invited our daughter and her first cousin (also celebrating her graduation) to travel with them. The party and the trip combined for a perfect way to make our daughter feel very special about graduating. These blessings settle within her heart a true sense of confidence and competence about entering adulthood.

Regardless of all the preparedness and celebrating of a child's independence, letting go is still difficult! When it is time to "release the arrow," may God help us all. If rites of passage are about preparing the child for independence, they are also very much about preparing the parent for "backing off" or "letting go." I think we (parents) need help, because for most of us, the "release" does not come naturally. Most college professors can tell you horror stories of what they call "helicopter moms." These are moms who "hover over" their college student son/daughter in a very suffocating way. Some parents call their college students daily, or even more often. They continue to help plan their every weekend and expect full participation with their family, as if the "child" lived at home. May God help you to prepare and bless and honor your young adult. May He reward your diligence as a parent with an adult child who follows in His ways and brings you joy. Ready. Aim. Fire!

BONUS - Using the Weekly Shabbat to Cultivate a Culture of Blessing in Your Family

"For as long as they were alive, my parents blessed me as the sun sank below the horizon each Friday evening. Since they were born, I have done the same for my children -- another link in the chain of blessing that God imparted to Abraham. This could enrich your family life for generations as it makes you part of an eternal chain." -- ***Rabbi Daniel Lapin***

Last Friday night, around the dinner table, my family sat eagerly waiting to eat. I looked Esther, my six year old, in the eye and spoke to her.

"Esther, you are fast. Smart. Pretty. Loving. You are helpful. Enthusiastic. Strong. Powerful. Fun. And I like you!"

My wife, Linette, and Esther's older brother and two older sisters said in unison, "And I like you too!"

Then as Esther continued to look into my eyes, I prayed with eyes open, "God, I thank you for Esther, my daughter. Thank you for the gift that she is to me and to my family. Thank you for filling her with a spirit of wisdom, knowledge, and understanding. Please cause these to increase within her. Thank you for helping her learn how to ride her bicycle with no training wheels. Empower her to know how much you love her. Fill Esther with Joy, and Peace, and Love, and Compassion. Help her to know your nearness, Lord. Surround her with favor and deliver her from evil and prosper her all the days of her life. Amen."

As I ended my prayer, Esther's face beamed with happiness and a big smile. I tore my gaze away from her wide, bright blue eyes to fix my gaze upon Elisha, my nine year old son. From the youngest to the oldest, I speak and pray blessings into the eyes of my children around the dinner table. This is how we begin most weekends.

This is the normal routine in our home. As we do this, we are joining thousands of Hebrew and Christian families around the globe and throughout the centuries in this Shabbat tradition of blessing the children. This idea of a father praying blessings for each child from the youngest to the oldest every Friday night around the supper table is an important part of the Jewish Shabbat ceremony. And I like it!

My friend Israel Fischer is an orthodox Jew who lives in New York. Israel and I have had many wonderful conversations about life and family. I have asked him to share his family tradition of Shabbat with you. As you read his story, consider what you can glean from Israel and how your family life can be enriched by incorporating Shabbat traditions in your weekend routine.

Israel Fischer - "How My Family Observes Shabbat"

The word "Shabbat" in Hebrew implies Rest. As the Bible tells us in Genesis, G-d created the Heavens and the Earth in six days, and rested on the seventh day. Shabbat is the most important ritual observance in Judaism. It is the only ritual observance instituted in the Ten Commandments.

Shabbat is not specifically a day of prayer. Although we do pray on Shabbat, and spend a substantial amount of time in the synagogue praying, prayer is not what distinguishes Shabbat from the rest of the week.

The mood is much like preparing for the arrival of a special, beloved guest: the house is cleaned, the family freshens and dresses up, the best dishes and tableware are set, and a festive meal is prepared. In addition, everything that cannot be done during Shabbat must be set up in advance: lights and appliances must be set (or timers placed on them), the light bulb in the refrigerator must be removed or unscrewed, so it does not turn on when you open it, and preparations for the remaining Shabbat meals must be made.

Shabbat begins at sundown Friday evening and is formally introduced by the lighting of candles. One candle is lit for each member of our family. At our household, we attend Shul (synagogue) services, after which we come back home and have a Shabbat dinner as a family. We begin the meal by reciting a blessing (referred to as "Kiddush") on a cup of wine or grape juice. The blessing, recited in Hebrew, explains the meaning and purpose of Shabbat.

Once we have all settled in, dinner officially starts! As a family, we sit at the table unbothered by any outside elements. The children recite Hebrew tunes. Throughout the course of the meal stories and anecdotes that highlight our heritage and instill our customary and traditional values to our children are shared. On occasion, the phone might ring, yet no one blinks an eye; probably a wrong number or perhaps a telemarketer. Sitting around the "Shabbat Table" is the one occasion throughout the week in which nothing really matters except "our family."

Each week we discuss topics of the current Weekly Torah portion. The older children identify with this very well, and it allows for some DMC's (Deep Meaningful Conversations) to happen. Everyone gets a chance to share their thoughts and insights of the past week, including hearing from my children what's going on at school. I truly see this as our primary medium for getting to know our kids better and to share in what is going on in their lives.

Saturday morning, after breakfast, we once again attend synagogue services. Once the services have finished, everyone, adults and children, meet and socialize with friends. It's a beautiful experience to gather and congregate with acquaintances and like-minded families, who all have the same values and feelings.

It's also a great opportunity for adults to gain some sanity. On Shabbat I don't engage in any business dealings -- no emails or phone calls to return. We typically don't discuss anything work-related or financial in nature. The daily pressures of our busy lives become non-existent for this holy twenty-four hours. The laundry and dishes won't get done, nor any other tasks or errands for that matter. The only chore and responsibility for the remainder of the day is rest and relaxation as a family.

Having grown up in a wonderful orthodox family all my life, I cannot imagine life without Shabbat. It's the one day when we recharge our spiritual, mental and physical batteries and begin the new week, more wholly integrated. We always find ourselves saying "Thank G-d for Shabbat!"

APPENDIX A
Sample Vows For A Blessing Ceremony

Vows by the honoree to the parents:

I, _____, promise to keep myself: my heart, soul and body, in wholeness and purity and singleness until I am married to my (husband/wife). I want you, my parents, to help me decide when is the right time for me to date, or spend significant time with a particular (man/woman). I promise to include you in conversations about my interests in a particular (man/woman). I want you to guide me in my decisions and in any commitments that I consider with someone. I will not make any plans or commitments to a (man/woman) or to a job or career without your agreement and support. I promise to keep you in the loop of my life decisions. With God's help.

Vows by parents to their honoree (in unison):

We, your mom and dad, promise to make ourselves available to you, to listen with our undivided attention whenever you ask. We recognize that you are now a (man/woman). We promise to treat you and your interests with respect and high regard. We want to protect you from unhealthy people and from dangerous situations. We promise to disclose to you our fears and concerns regarding your interests. We promise to keep you in the loop of our life decisions. With God's help.

Vows by the audience to parents and honoree (parents ask the audience to stand to their feet and say this vow in unison):

I acknowledge _____(honoree's name) as a new adult.   We welcome (him/her) into our fellowship as a young adult in our midst. With God's help.

APPENDIX B
Driving Contract

I, _____, understand that driving is a privilege, not a right. I understand that driving is dangerous, and that traffic accidents are the number one killer of teenagers in America. When I get into my car, I will pray and ask God to help me stay alert and keep me safe and deliver me from evil. I enter into this driving contract with _____ my parents.

___I agree to study and learn the driving rules and regulations of my state. I agree to obey all traffic laws.

___I agree to refrain from using a cell phone, texting, or holding an MP3 player while driving. I will pull off the road into a parking lot before using these while I am in the car. I will not take my eyes off of the road to change a radio setting or play a CD, etc.

I will follow my parent's rules and guidelines for driving:

___I will not drive with more than _____ passengers in my car without a parent or other adult in the car with me.

___I will not drive at night later than _____ o'clock pm.

___I will not drive with anyone in the car who is under the influence of alcohol or another drug. I will not drink alcohol or use any other drug. I will not drive under the influence of alcohol or any drug. If I ever break this promise I will call home for help and not drive.

___When driving, I will keep both hands on the wheel and both eyes on the road at all times.

___I will not rush, or speed, or hurry when driving.

___I will slow down at yellow lights, always signal before turning, and stop at stop signs and red lights.

___I will not tailgate. I will keep a minimum of one car distance per every ten miles per hour of speed between me and another moving vehicle in front of me, and a minimum of being able to see the rear tires of the vehicle stopped in front of me in traffic or at an intersection.

___I understand that driving defensively means that it is my responsibility to prevent accidents by driving extra cautiously. Even when I legally have the right of way, I understand that it is better to be safe and yield to the other vehicle, than to be right about my right of way and contribute to an accident.

___ I will not drive with an empty gas tank, or a flat tire. I will call Mom or Dad first for help if I have a flat tire, or run out of gas, or have an accident or any other car problems.

___I will change the oil every 3,000 miles. I will check the oil every time I fill up with gas and keep the oil gauge at full at all times.

___I will not take chances or risks when I drive.

I commit myself to these agreements and promises. I understand that my parents may remove or limit my driving privileges for breaking any of these agreements. I understand that arguing about any of these agreements or any driving request or driving limitation from either of my parents is unacceptable and will jeopardize my driving privileges immediately.

_____(teenager signature)

I acknowledge that my parents are experienced drivers and have valuable instruction and guidance for my safety as a driver. I want to learn from my parents and gladly agree to every item in this driving contract. I am thankful for the privilege to drive.

_____ (teenager signature)

I, _____(parent),

give you, _____(teen), the privilege to
drive according to the terms of this driving contract. I expect you
to keep the terms of this contract. I expect you to disclose to me
times when you break this contract. I will pray for your safety
and ask God to deliver you from evil. I will help you become a
skilled, experienced and safe driver.

_____(parent's signature)

APPENDIX C
One Dad's Letter to his Thirteen Year Old Son

Eli John Paul,

Today you turn thirteen. It's as good an excuse as any to recognize a shift in life, a movement from boyhood to young manhood, a rite of passage. Of course, life is never that black and white, as if we'll all notice a drastic change from yesterday to today, but at a minimum, something IS happening in you and to you. And it is good.

First, let me say that YOU ARE AWESOME!! There's nobody like you (exactly like you) — never has been, never will be. You're one of kind. Now before you go thinking you're uniquely more special than anyone else, you live in a world with six billion other "one-of-a-kinds!" But it's important to understand your uniqueness — your strengths and weaknesses, where you rock and where you reek. Know when it's your time to step up or back down, to speak up or shut up, to get involved or to withdraw. You will learn by trying, by taking risks; and this is a very painful method, but it's the only way. Give yourself room to fail, keep trying, don't be too hard on yourself, don't beat yourself up. Like yourself. Love yourself. And remember your mother and I love you and always will.

So here's some advice…

Be YOU.

Son, I absolutely love the young man you're becoming, watching you these last twelve years. While some people are comfortable copying the lives of others, I see that you're doing a remarkable job being yourself. With so much life ahead of you, there will be lots of influences. The brave new world will try to tell you what you should do, how to do it, and what to become, but be you. You don't have to be the cool guy or a part of the in-crowd. If people do not accept you for who you are, it's their loss for not recognizing someone as authentic and interesting as you. Be you and you will attract people.

Find Your Own Values And Live By Them.

No one knows everything and no one ever will, but as you go, you will discover and form a strong set of core values — things you believe in. These values may change as you are exposed to more and more life and circumstances. Life has a way of teaching many lessons. It's as if God has each person on an IEP (Individual Educational Plan)...teaching us only what we can grasp at each stage of life. Life will force you to make decisions, and your values will point the way. As you define your personal core values, you will build strong character and cultivate yourself as a good man, living a good life on an upward trajectory of better and better.

Now Do.

Out of your self-awareness and self-love will flow expressions of your passions and your causes. Because your heart is pure, your values, passions, and causes will end up benefitting your community, your country, your life, your friends and humanity. Go places to see different cultures and meet regularly with people who are different. Reach out to life by being active; volunteer where it's needed. Life is about what we do for others.

Life Is Not A Race

You seem to already have this down, but its worth saying anyway. Live life one day at a time -- don't rush it, celebrate the small victories in life and keep moving forward. Take your time, run at a steady pace, work your plan, and the desires of you heart will come into your life in due time. Remember that with each step you take in life you must give your personal best.

Be Strong

Being strong for a man means physical strength AND internal strength -- will power, resiliency, confidence, and standing up for what you believe. Grow thicker skin so you're not easily offended. When you feel that it's almost time to quit, don't. Dig deep and fight through it.

Set Backs

Life is one big crazy rodeo; things can go so well one day and the next you'll find yourself knocked to the ground. I say to you get up, dust yourself off and look for no one's pity. Get back on and ride again, only this time you're wiser. Your ability to bounce back from setbacks will keep you moving forward on your life's journey. Do not "should" on yourself or allow shame to crush you. Get up -- life happens to everyone. The same rain, the same sun fall on the righteous and the unrighteous.

Love

This is the most important thing in the universe. Look for it. Let it fill your heart. Love cares more for others than for self. It doesn't want what it doesn't have. Love doesn't strut, doesn't have a swelled head, doesn't force itself on others, isn't always "me first," doesn't fly off the handle, doesn't keep score of others' mistakes. It's happy for the happy and sad for the sad, puts up with anything, always looks for the best, never looks back, keeps going to the end.

Son, you're an amazing young man. You have tremendous gifts. Remember that your life is supposed to work, and you have the wind of all who love you in your sails. You are ready for this next phase. You have what it takes. And you are loved and supported by many friends and family.

Love,
Dad

Personal Stories

The second half of this book has not yet been written. I need your help! I would love to publish your story of blessing. I want stories from fathers, mothers, young men, young women, old men, and old women! Once you have experienced your own blessing ceremony, or any one of the rites of passage recommended in this book, then please share it with me. If I print your story in a future edition of this book, I will pay you a nominal fee.

Please feel free to send me your story as a letter or in any form that you choose. If you want some help of "where to start," then I have provided this guide for you, but only as a suggestion.

Summary Guide

1. Begin with the fondest recollection of your event. Describe the memories that first come to mind from your blessing ceremony. Highlights: what you wore, who was there, what you ate, the decorations, what was spoken, or sung, etc. -- anything that you remember with fondness about your rite of passage/blessing ceremony. Describe the order of your ceremony: what happened first, second, ... last, etc.

2. What role did you play in the ceremony? Share any details you remember about your speech or anything else you did.

3. How did you feel after it was over? What did this ceremony mean to you?

4. Describe any regrets. If you could do it over again, what would you change?

Email your story to *blessings@huntermcfarlin.com* or visit my website, *www.huntermcfarlin.com*, to upload your pdf file. I would prefer to receive your story in the body of your email, or as a pdf file. If you do not know how to create a pdf, one way to do so is by using "cutepdf." Just go to *www.cutepdf.com.* This is a free download. It makes *cutepdf* one of your printer choices, then you just print your story, choose *cutepdf* as your printer and *voilà*!

Or feel free to mail me your handwritten stories to:

Hunter McFarlin
119 N. Maple Street
Murfreesboro, TN 37130

FEEDBACK

If you experience good results from this book and want to recommend it to others, please email me your quote or paragraph of recommendation. Or you may have suggestions or tips for other parents or teenagers. Please give me your feedback! Send me an email -- *blessings@huntermcfarlin.com* or visit my website: *www.huntermcfarlin.com.*

CPSIA information can be obtained at www.ICGtesting.com
Printed in the USA
BVOW031730130312

285106BV00006B/8/P